MIRACLES
of Forgiveness

WHEN MIRACLES HAPPEN
True Stories of God's Divine Touch

Edited by Mary Hollingsworth

Guideposts Books
Carmel, New York

Acknowledgments

Every attempt has been made to credit the sources of copyrighted material used in this book. If any such acknowledgment has been inadvertently omitted or miscredited, receipt of such information would be appreciated.

All material that originally appeared in Guideposts publicatons is reprinted with permission. Copyright © Guideposts, Carmel, NY.

Unless otherwise noted, Scripture quotations are from the Holy Bible, New International Version. Copyright © 1973, 1978, 1984, International Bible Society. Used by permission of Zondervan Bible Publishers.

Quotations designated NCV are from the New Century Version®. Copyright © 1987, 1988, 1991 by Thomas Nelson, Inc. All rights reserved.

Quotations designated NASB are from the New American Standard Bible, © 1960, 1977 by the Lockman Foundation.

Quotations designated TEV are from the Good News Bible: The Bible in Today's English Version, © 1976 by the American Bible Society.

"The St. Patrick's Day Fiasco" and "Why Misti?" published by permission from *Whispers from Heaven*, copyright © Publications International, Ltd.

"The St. Patrick's Day Fiasco" and "Why Misti?" published by permission from *Whispers from Heaven*, copyright © Publications International, Ltd. "The Answer" from A Touch of Wonder by Arthur Gordon (Grand Rapids: Fleming H. Revell, a division of Baker Publishing Group, 1974). Used by permission. "The Power of Touch" from Gathered Stones by Michael L. Lyle (Victoria, BC: Trafford Publishing, 2005). "Forgiveness Brings Healing" from Miracles Still Happen by Sheri Stone and Therese Marszalek (Tulsa, OK: Harrison House, 2003). Used by permission of authors.

"Lost and Found" by Christine Royle as told to BJ Taylor, "Fussing, Fighting, and Forgiving" by Phillip Gulley, "What Happened" by Naomi Lederach, "A Scrapbook of Forgiveness" by Darlene Franklin, "Unexpected Forgiveness" by Pamela R. Watts, "I Walk by Faith" by Christopher Harvey as told to Vie Herlocker, "Ice Cream for My Kids" by Debbie Davis as told to Gene Shelburne, "Football and Forgiveness" by Rachael Philips, "Let Bygones Be Bygones" by Renie (Szilak) Burghardt, "Last Request" by Zarette Beard, "Forgiveness with a Hitch" by Patti Maguire Armstrong, "An Old Rotary Dial Telephone" by Nancy B. Gibbs, "My Trusted Friend" by Joanne K. Hill, "The Road to Forgiveness" by Holly Baxley, "Finding Life on Death Row" by Sue Norton as told to Aba Gayle, and "The Circle of Forgiveness" by BJ Taylor; are used by permission of the authors.

Editorial, research, and content development managed by Shady Oaks Studio, Bedford, Texas. Team members: Patty Crowley, Rhonda Hogan, Mary Hollingsworth, Mary Kay Knox, Kathryn Murray, Nancy Sullivan, Stephanie Terry, and Barbara Tork.

www.guideposts.org
(800) 431-2344
Guideposts Books & Inspirational Media Division
Designed by Jerry O'Brien
Illustrations by Ron Bucalo
Jacket design and photo by The DesignWorks Group, Inc.

Printed in the United States of America

Contents

≈≈≈≈

⨠⨠⨠

CHAPTER 2 RECLAIMING HEARTS

CHAPTER 3 REPAIRING RELATIONSHIPS

CHAPTER 4 RECEIVING PEACE

CHAPTER 5 REDEEMING THE LOST

Introduction

Forgiveness. Perhaps the most important concept in all of the Bible. We all need it desperately. And God's entire plan for our redemption is centered around it. He even gave His only Son to help us achieve it.

Forgiveness is a word we love to *hear* but hate to *practice*. We love to *receive* it, but we hate to have to *give* it. It may be the most difficult command in God's Word. But without forgiveness life is impossible in the long run and chaotic in the short run. It's the oil that keeps the wheels of life turning smoothly.

Forgiveness often comes slowly and through much pain and struggle. When given freely, though, it's a wonderful thing to behold. At times it's even miraculous, as the stories in *Miracles of Forgiveness* will demonstrate.

After being shot in the head and going blind, Chris found a way to move on with his life by forgiving the shooter in Chapter One that deals with "Restoring Hope." Michael discovers the power of touch when his tiny premature baby shows him hope for the future. And Frances has a chance to forgive a mugger who attacks her.

In Chapter Two, "Reclaiming Hearts," Christine blames God for the deaths of two important men in her life, and then learns to trust Him again through forgiveness. Leilani is left standing alone on the dance floor at her wedding by her father, but a substitute father steps in and shows her how to reclaim that relationship. And Darlene released her bitterness by giving her ex-husband a gift.

"Repairing Relationships" is a critical part of life as we see in Chapter Three when Rachael chooses to spend her dwindling funds on football tickets to be close to her love. Renie's grandfather shows the beauty of forgiveness when he accepts the apologies of the man who tried to have him arrested in Hungary during World War II. And Patti learns that forgiveness must be given without a hitch.

In Chapter Four we find the joy of "Receiving Peace" through forgiveness. Mary's mistake leads to the permanent disability of her toddler son, but she eventually allows God's forgiveness to quiet her mind and heart. Nancy discovers peace through an old rotary dial telephone. And Joanne found peace in forgiving her cantankerous grandmother.

Chapter Five, "Redeeming the Lost," finds Rob able to walk again after forgiving someone he thought he could never forgive. And Robert receives an unexpected touch of grace when he is healed through prayer—truly a miracle of forgiveness.

All the stories in this book are true. They give us glimpses of the glory of God as He sheds His marvelous light into the world through the forgiveness His children share with the world. Perhaps you, too, will see His glory as you turn the pages.

MARY HOLLINGSWORTH

MIRACLES

of Forgiveness

CHAPTER 1

Restoring Hope

Why am I so sad? Why am I so upset? I should put my hope in God and keep praising him, my Savior and my God (Psalm 42:5–6 NCV).

Forgiveness reaches into the past and restores lost hopes and dreams destroyed by unkind words, cantankerous spirits, or spiteful actions. Forgiveness can erase mistakes we've made, calm troubled waters, and bring God's light back into seemingly hopeless situations. It's the gentle touch of God's love that puts upside down life right side up again.

My Bitter Heart

RITA ROSKAM

"Guess where I've been," my husband, Ron, said as he walked in the door one spring evening. Without waiting for an answer, he told me, "I went to see my mother." He must have noticed the shocked look on my face, because he admitted, "I know. I can't believe it myself."

I wanted to ask why he had gotten in touch with that woman after so many years, especially when he could hardly bear to hear her name mentioned. But as I had learned to do with almost every other question I'd had about his childhood, I left this one alone. Ron had already been through enough in his life. The last thing I wanted was to make him relive a time he found too painful to talk about.

Even before we started dating back in tenth grade in Comanche, Oklahoma, I had sensed there was something different about Ron, more complicated somehow than the other boys in school. I began to understand when, after we'd been going together a while, he told me that the folks he'd introduced as his mom and dad had adopted him. All he said by way of explanation was that his birth mother had abandoned him when he was three years old. The rest I learned from old newspapers his adoptive mother had saved. Perhaps I shouldn't have delved into Ron's past, but I couldn't help it. I wanted to know what was behind the hurt I saw deep in his eyes.

The more I read, the more I wondered what kind of woman could have treated her children, her own flesh and blood, so terribly. Ron and his brothers and sisters had been found in a run-down house with no heat or electricity, no adults to look after them. The oldest was five; the youngest, just an infant. Ron was curled up in a pile of dirty clothes, trying to keep warm. The children were hospitalized and treated for malnutrition. Their father couldn't take care of them any better than their mother, so they went into foster homes, and were later adopted by different families.

It never ceased to amaze me that Ron had been able to put all that behind him and grow up to be a gentle, caring man, a minister whose greatest joy was helping other people. My prayer after Ron and I married was, *Lord, show me how to ease his hurt. Help me give him all the love he's missed out on.* Sometimes when I held one of our children in my arms, I'd see Ron watching us tenderly, and with an ache in my heart, I'd remember, *No one did this for him.* Yet Ron was so wonderful with our three kids, and it made me love him all the more—for how hard he worked to be a good father, how he'd risen above the pain of his past.

So that spring evening I didn't push when he didn't say anything else about his visit with his mother. But as we lay in bed that night, my head resting on his shoulder, he began, for the first time since I'd known him, to talk about her.

"Seeing Peggy wasn't anything like I'd expected," he said. "I thought I'd feel something for her, but I might as well have been speaking to a perfect stranger. She looked old and used-up, with scars all over her face like she must have been beaten a lot. The man she's married to now was there, and you know, she had the gall to tell him, 'At least one of my kids amounted to something.'"

I lay there quietly and listened, watching the moonlight play across his face. He looked so vulnerable, and once again I found myself thinking, *What a hurt little boy lives inside this man of mine . . .*

Ron did not talk about Peggy after that night, and as usual, I left the subject untouched. Once in a while he'd get kind of withdrawn, and I'd wonder if he was brooding on the fact that his own mother hadn't wanted him.

Three years after that visit with her, Ron got a call from one of his brothers. Peggy was sick and had only weeks to live. "She'd like a chance to get to know you better," his brother said.

"I'll have to think about it," Ron replied. I knew that we would end up going to see her.

One sunny Saturday morning Ron and I drove to Peggy's. It turned out she didn't live far from where we'd gone to high school. Her house was small and narrow, and when we stepped inside, the air seemed stale, as if it had been a long time since she'd been able to take care of the place properly.

Ron and I sat beside Peggy's sickbed. He introduced me, and they started chatting, a little awkwardly. I didn't notice what they were saying because all I could focus on was Peggy's face. I couldn't tear my eyes away. Ron looked so much like her!

Anger coursed through me. How could you turn your back on someone who's so clearly a part of you? I wanted to scream at Peggy. I heard Ron telling her about our kids, but in my head their conversation was drowned out by a torrent of thoughts whose bitterness surprised me. *How could you hurt your little boy when all he wanted from you was love? A mother who would do that . . . well, maybe you deserve to spend your last days alone.*

I couldn't stop myself from thinking these awful things. I was relieved when Ron said, "Peggy, I can see you're tired. Rita and I will be going now, but we'll be back."

Every time we went to visit her, I struggled with my feelings. I admired how she never lost her sense of humor even when her body was failing her. At the same time, I could not forget what she had done to her children, to the man I loved. Ron seemed to be handling the situation well. He was still careful to call her Peggy, not Mom, but his manner toward her was calm, accepting. I was the one burning up inside.

Peggy became too weak to take care of herself. Whenever we could, Ron and I and his siblings and their spouses looked after her—feeding her, changing her bedding, giving her medication. I busied myself with these chores, as if redirecting all the anger I felt toward her into some concrete activity meant I wouldn't have to think about it. I wasn't so much helping her as trying not to hate her.

One afternoon while we were over, Peggy said, "Well, some of you showed up to see your momma go. That's better than I expected."

That's better than you deserve. Where were you when Ron needed to be taken care of? Where were you all those times he cried because no one loved him and he had no place to call home?

I caught myself. *Lord, what's wrong with me?* Here was Ron, promising the woman who had abandoned him as a child that he wouldn't let her die alone. If Ron could give so much, I could at least try to give a little— for him. *Maybe I won't ever be able to love her, Lord, but help me overcome my bitter heart.*

A few days later, we got word that Peggy had been admitted to the hospital. She lapsed into a coma, and we took turns sitting with her. One day everyone else went to the waiting room to take a break. I was alone with Peggy. My eyes moved over her gaunt frame and came to rest on her face. As with the first time I had met her, I couldn't wrench my gaze away. There was a remarkable likeness to Ron. To our son and daughters.

Suddenly it dawned on me: I had carried her very blood in my womb. Peggy was a part of me, a part of the people who meant the most to me—my husband and children. She had given me more than I'd realized. Despite her mistakes, she had given me Ron, the man I loved just as he was, complications and all.

The nurses came to turn Peggy in bed. As they moved her, she cried out in her sleep. All at once I wanted to cry for her, for all the pain she was going through now. And for all that she must have gone through in the past that had made her unable to show her own children love.

When the nurses left, I leaned close to Peggy. "I'm sorry that you're suffering," I said. "I'm sorry that I felt you deserved this. I don't know what went wrong all those years ago, and I won't even pretend to understand, but I want to thank you for Ron. I wish you could have really gotten to see what a good father—and a wonderful husband—he is. No matter what has happened, Peggy, you are his mother, and I want you to know I love you because of that."

I bent to kiss her cheek. Her eyes fluttered open, then just as quickly, closed again. Her breathing became raspy, labored. I ran into the lobby and told everyone to come quick. Back in Peggy's room, a nurse was examining her. "It won't be long now," the nurse said, shaking her head. "I'm sorry."

Ron touched Peggy's arm, and his lips moved, but no sound came out. Then, in a voice so small that I had to listen closely to be sure it had come from him, he whispered, "Momma, I forgive you."

I watched as he stayed by her side while her breathing slowed. Peggy and Ron, mother and son, so connected and yet so separate, so alike and yet so different, coming together only at the beginning of his life and the ending of hers.

Finally Peggy gave a long sigh and was gone. Ron bowed his head for a moment, then looked up at me. Our eyes met.

I could still see the little boy in the man I loved. Only now I saw how he was healing. And how I was too.

I Walk by Faith

CHRISTOPHER HARVEY

I slid into the wingback chair in Grandmother's living room, my feet barely reaching the floor.

"Christopher Harvey! Why don't you go to the basement and play with your brother and cousins? Let us adults have our own time together. Go on, scoot!"

"Aw, Mom, please . . . I'll go in a few minutes."

"Let the boy stay a while, although I do declare, for a nine-year-old he wants to grow up too fast."

Wants to grow up too fast, wants to grow up too fast. Grandmother's words rolled around in my head like a pinball that suddenly found its mark. I didn't really *want* to grow up fast; I *had* to grow up fast. That was part of the feeling. I couldn't put words to the feeling. It wasn't scary, just a sense of knowing that I was somehow different, and that my adulthood would not be normal.

Throughout childhood this feeling continued to well up inside of me. It created a sense of urgency that compelled me to seek a world of self-sufficiency and independence. With a child's perception I knew the feeling was from God. But how could a child explain that to anyone?

Through the years, though, I found myself thinking less about God and more about my own desires and ambitions. When the feeling recurred, I rationalized it as part of my personality. It spurred my need to be the very best in everything I attempted.

I didn't think about the feeling much after I graduated from high school and entered Shepherd College in West Virginia. Then, in the second semester of my junior year, it happened again. I wanted the added freedom of living off campus; so the opportunity to move into a rental house in nearby Sharpsburg, Maryland, with my friend Hutch was perfect. On moving day, I arrived with my belongings on a borrowed pick-up truck, opened the tailgate to begin unloading, and was overwhelmed with an unsettling feeling. It was the feeling from childhood, but this time it seemed foreboding.

Feeling or no feeling, the move off campus satisfied my need for more control over my own life. As the semester ended, I eagerly anticipated a summer at the beach.

It was around nine o'clock in the evening when I parked my white Maverick in front of the aging clapboard house and bounded up the front porch steps.

Hutch wasn't home yet, so it was the ideal quiet time to study for my next exam. But my mind was racing. I was on top of the world. In a few days I would be back at the same job I had last summer, managing the meat department at 64th Street Market, right next to the bridge in

Ocean City. My school year had gone well. I was nominated for Who's Who in America's Colleges. I maintained a 3.4 grade point average without denting my social life. I pledged Lambda Chi Alpha in the fall and was elected vice president.

Everything was going my way. I knew what I wanted out of life, and I went after it with fervor. If my adult life was going to be different in some way, I wanted to be the one to shape it.

I made a roast beef sandwich, gathered my economics notes, and headed to the living room, determined to get some studying done before Hutch arrived home. I flipped on the ceiling light, as well as our prized orange-globed swag light. Even with both lights on, the dark barn-wood paneling made the room dim. We liked it that way.

I placed my notes and sandwich on the coffee table and plopped down on the ratty old couch. We'd covered it with an orange-and-brown-paisley throw to match the swag light. Someone had given us a yellow accent pillow, which I tossed from the couch into the dingy white platform rocker across the room. Now I was ready to tackle my studies.

About 11:30 PM Hutch arrived and joined me in the living room. "Think fast, man!" He grabbed the pillow out of the rocker and threw it at me like a football.

I caught the pillow and then put it and my notes aside. As we talked about our summer plans, our conversation stopped when we heard a series of loud pops and bangs outside.

"What was that?" Hutch's voice reflected the fear I felt.

I sat upright and motionless on the edge of the couch, starring ahead at the white doorframe, which separated the living room from the parlor. The frame seemed to glow against the dark paneling as I waited for the next sound, hoping to figure out where it was coming from.

Suddenly, the wall to the left of the couch erupted, and I felt as if I had been slammed in the head with a baseball bat. The force swung me around and threw me backwards.

Oh, God, help me!

I could feel and taste warm blood running down my throat and pouring down my face. I groped for the pillow, pressed it to my face, and lay flat on the couch.

I called out for Hutch.

"Stay down!" he yelled back to me. I heard him pulling himself along the floor to the phone, which was just inside the parlor.

"Help us, please! I think my roomie's been shot—hurry, you've got to help us! Yes, OK, yes, it's 221 W. Antietam Street. Yes! I don't know! There were bangs—please, just send help fast! He's bleeding around his head! He's bleeding badly! I can't keep talking! Help us!"

He slammed the receiver down and slid back across the floor to the couch. "Help's coming, Chris. You're going to be OK."

I was in pain and slipping into shock, but I had to ask, "Hutch, I've got to know something. Is part of my face gone?" I pulled the pillow away.

"No, man, you're all right, you're all right. Everything is there."

"Hutch, tell me the truth; don't lie to me!"

"You've got blood all over your face, but everything is there."

"I can't see any light."

"Look man, lay back down! There's blood all over your eyes, but you're all right!"

I wanted to believe him. I didn't feel all right; it felt like the whole front of my face was gone. I pressed the pillow back to my face, trying to stop the gushing blood.

God, please don't let this be as bad as I think it is. Help me. Please help me.

Calmness enveloped me and I immediately made the connection with my childhood feeling. I knew, without a doubt, that God had planted a seed within my heart years ago to prepare me for an adulthood that would be different in some way. That instant, that moment in time was what God had been preparing me for since childhood.

I became aware of the hollow sound of sirens as the ambulance made its way through the streets to our house. As I heard the ambulance turn down our street, I had the sensation of leaving my body.

I floated above the living room, looking down.

Instead of the four walls, I peered into a circular area. Darkness surrounded the circle, yet it teemed with star-like pinpoints of light. The front door burst open and I watched the paramedics come in. The first one grabbed the rocking chair and flung it aside. The next paramedic, wearing a dark-gray firefighter's jacket, bent over and removed the coffee table. I saw more paramedics bring the stretcher into the room. My attention moved briefly to the couch, and I watched as they placed my body onto the stretcher. Then my awareness faded. I came to, back in my body, as they were taking the stretcher down the steps of the front porch.

I remember being in the emergency room waiting for a doctor to examine me. A strong antiseptic odor hung in the room, and the taste of blood lingered in my throat.

When the doctor arrived, he determined that a bullet had entered the corner of my left eye, and I had no vision in either eye. He did not know if the bullet had exited or was lodged in my brain. The nurses then prepped me for an airlift to the Johns Hopkins Medical Center Shock Trauma Unit. Since the only helicopter available was too small to accommodate a stretcher, they strapped me in a bubble on the landing skid.

The jerky movement of the vertical take-off startled me, and I grabbed the edges of the stretcher. A tangle of wires, monitoring my vital signs, passed through a small opening in the bubble and into the helicopter. The chop of the blades became background to the whistle of the wind passing over that opening as the craft changed to forward motion.

Just a few hours earlier, I was on top of the world. I was in control. Now I was suspended above the world, helpless and alone. Alone, except for God.

I knew God had been with me all of my life, yet I had put Him in the background and lived for my own selfish purposes. As I called out to God now, peacefulness surrounded me. He was in control and had been even when I didn't choose to see Him. If I lived or if I died, the call was His, not mine.

While the helicopter hovered over the landing pad at Johns Hopkins, I placed my future in God's loving hands. I accepted that my life would be different from that moment on, and I knew that He had already prepared me. He had been with me all along, and He would not leave me now.

Dr. Lawrence Hirst, the top surgeon at Hopkins' Wilmer Eye Clinic examined me and confirmed that I was blind and had been from the moment of injury. A bullet fragment had entered the corner of my left eye, traveled behind the bridge of my nose, and exited out the corner of my right eye, severing my optic nerves. My eyes would have to be surgically removed. I learned that my injury was the result of a drunken young man shooting at houses and parked vehicles with a 30–30 Marlin hunting rifle. At a time when anger and bitterness would have normally overwhelmed me, I felt peace. God had so prepared me for this that I instantly forgave the young man who shot me. My life would never be the same, but I knew God was in control.

After my release from the hospital, my family employed private Braille and mobility instructors. In six weeks of intensive study, I completed the equivalent of two years of Braille training. A little more than three months after the shooting, I returned to the house in Sharpsburg and resumed classes at Shepherd College. I graduated, Cum Laude, with my class in the spring of 1981.

I went on to graduate school at the University of Virginia, where I was the first blind person to receive the M.A. degree from the economics department and now serve as first vice president/investments and a certified portfolio manager for Salomon Smith Barney. I have a speaking ministry reflecting God's faithfulness in helping me deal with blindness. It's my desire that my testimony might be an encouragement to others.

I am often asked how I was able to forgive the young man who shot me. I was blessed by my Creator with the grace to be able to forgive him, even though he never apologized. I almost instantly forgave him for that incident. What is important about forgiveness is that it allows you to move on with your life. It allows you to free yourself up from bitterness, resentment, hatred, dislike, and unproductivity.

It has been more than twenty-five years since that night in Sharpsburg. I lost my sight in the prime of my life—blinded with no hope of restored physical vision. Instead, I was given a vision of new hope through total dependence on God. The feeling that I had since childhood became reality that night. My headstrong spirit, which resulted from the feeling and had driven me to personal gain became the sustaining spirit that never let me give up as God taught me to deal with a lifetime disability. Since then, I have been blessed with a devoted wife, three children, and a rewarding career. But the best blessing of all has been the daily walk, not by sight, but by faith in my wise and loving God.

The Answer

ARTHUR GORDON

T he day had been long and hot. Some of us had spent most of it struggling with one of those civil rights problems that plague American towns from time to time. It had all been painfully familiar: the mayor listening in troubled silence; the surface politeness masking the deep grievances; the helpless feeling of having left the old simple right-or-wrong far behind and then reached the arid region where right clashes endlessly with right.

I came home tired and discouraged. "At times it seems hopeless," I said dejectedly to my wife. "The wounds are too old; the scar tissue is too thick. There just isn't any answer."

She was standing at the kitchen sink making a salad. "Oh, I don't know," she said. "I heard a pretty good answer today down at the hospital."

(As a hospital volunteer, my wife pushes a cart full of magazines and paperbacks. She talks to patients, and patients talk to her. Sometimes bored or lonely they tell her all sorts of things about themselves.) In this case, she

said the editor of a small country newspaper was conva-
lescing from an operation. She dried her hands on a dish
towel.

"You ought to stop by and let him tell you the story
he told me. I think you'd be impressed."

"Why can't you tell me what he said?" I asked.

"It wouldn't be the same. You ought to get it from
him."

And so the next day I stopped by the hospital. The
patient was still there, padding around in a dressing
gown and slippers—a tall man with gentle blue eyes and
a gift for words. We sat in the visitors' lounge, and this
is the story he had to tell . . .

I was a timid six-year-old with braces on my
legs—a frail, lost, lonely little boy when I first
arrived at the farm in Georgia. Had it not been for
an extraordinary woman, I might have remained
that way.

She lived on the farm in a two-room cabin
where her parents had been slaves. To an out-
sider she looked like any of the black people on
the place in her shapeless gray dress. But to those
who knew her she was a spiritual force whose
influence was felt everywhere.

She was the first person called when there
was sickness; she made medicines from roots and

herbs that seemed to cure just about anything. She had a family of her own, but all of the children around felt that somehow they belonged to her. Her name reflected this. In the soft speech of the Georgia lowlands the word *maum* is a slurred version of *mama*. We called her Maum Jean.

Maum Jean talked to the Lord often and we all suspected that when she did, He stopped whatever He was doing, listened, and took appropriate action. Her heart reached out to small, helpless things, so she took particular interest in me from the start.

When I was stricken with polio at the age of three, I'm sure my parents didn't know what was the matter with me. All they knew was that times were hard and suddenly they had a crippled child on their hands. They took me to a New York City hospital, left me, and never came back. The people who took me into their foster home had relatives on the Georgia estate where I was sent in hopes that the warmer climate might help.

Maum Jean's sensitive emotional antenna instantly picked up the loneliness and withdrawal inside me, just as her marvelous diagnostic sense surveyed the polio damage and decided that, regardless of what the doctors might have said, something more ought to be done. Maum Jean had never heard the word *atrophy*, but she knew that muscles could waste away unless used. And so every night when her tasks were done she would come to my room and kneel beside my bed to massage my legs.

Sometimes, when I would cry out with pain, she would sing old songs or tell me stories. When her treatments were over, she would always talk earnestly to the Lord, explaining that she was doing what she could but that she would need help, and when the day came she wanted Him to give her a sign.

A creek wound through the farm and Maum Jean, who had never heard of hydrotherapy, said there was strength in running water. She made her grandsons carry me down to a sandy bank where I could splash around pretty well.

Slowly I grew taller, but there was little change in my legs. I still used crutches; I still buckled on the clumsy braces. Night after night Maum Jean continued the massaging and praying. Then one morning, when I was about twelve, she told me she had a surprise for me.

She led me out into the yard and placed me with my back against an oak tree; I can feel the rough bark of it to this day. She took away my crutches and braces. She moved back a dozen paces and told me that the Lord had spoken to her in a dream. He had said that the time had come for me to walk. "So now," said Maum Jean, "I want you to walk over here to me."

My instant reaction was fear. I knew I couldn't walk unaided; I had tried. I shrank back against the solid support of the tree. Maum Jean continued to urge me.

I burst into tears. I begged. I pleaded. Her voice rose suddenly, no longer gentle and coaxing but full of power and command. "You can walk, boy! The Lord has spoken! Now walk over here."

She knelt down and held out her arms. And somehow, impelled by something stronger than fear, I took a faltering step, and another, and another, until I reached Maum Jean and fell into her arms, both of us weeping.

It was two more years before I could walk normally, but I never used the crutches again. For a while longer I lived in my twilight world, halfway between the whites, who considered me part alien, and the blacks, who could offer affection but no kinship. Then a circus came through town, and when it left, I left with it.

For the next few years I worked with one circus or another. Now and then, when the circus went into winter quarters, I would come back to the little town and help the editor of the weekly newspaper. There was little money in it, but I liked the smell of ink and the sound of words. I never went back to the farm; a runaway seldom returns. But I always asked about Maum Jean, and when I could afford it I sent her little things.

Then the night came when one of Maum Jean's tall grandsons knocked on my door. It was late; there was frost in the air. Maum Jean was dying, he said; she wanted to see me.

The old cabin was unchanged: floors of cypress, windows with wooden shutters—no glass, roof of palm thatch mixed with pitch. Maum Jean lay in bed surrounded by silent watchers, her frail body covered by a patchwork quilt. From a corner of the room, a kerosene lamp cast a dim saffron light. Her face was in shadow, but I heard her whisper my name. Someone put a chair close to the bed. I sat down and touched her hand.

For a long time I sat there. Around me the dark faces were grave and patient. There were no tears, no chants, all was quiet. Now and then Maum Jean spoke softly. Her mind was clear. She hoped I remembered the things she had taught me. Outside, the night wind stirred. In the other room the fire snapped, throwing orange sparks. There was a long silence; she lay with her eyes closed. Then the old voice spoke, stronger suddenly. "Oh," said Maum Jean with surprise and gladness, "It's so *beautiful!*" She gave a little contented sigh and died.

And then something quite unbelievable happened: in the semidarkness her face seemed to glow. No one had touched the lamp. There was no other source of light. But her features, which had been almost invisible, could be seen plainly, and she was smiling. It lasted for perhaps ten seconds. It was most strange, but not at all frightening. I couldn't account for it then, and I can't account for it now. But I saw it. We all saw it. Then it faded and was gone . . .

My companion stopped speaking. In the corridor I heard the rattle of an instrument cart as a nurse hurried by. Finally he spoke again.

"All that happened a long time ago. I live in another town now. But I still think of Maum Jean often and the main thing she taught me: nothing is a barrier when love is strong enough. Not age. Not race. Not anything."

I took a deep breath, remembering what my wife had said. The answer? Maybe someday. Someday. . . .

The Power of Touch

MICHAEL L. LYLE

Having just left my wife in a hospital across town, I stood in the lobby of another hospital, one with a neonatal intensive care unit, looking for the admitting area. I needed to admit our newborn daughter, and then I needed to find her. I've never been more afraid. I believed my wife would survive, but feared that our daughter would not.

Early in the pregnancy, my wife *just knew* something wasn't right. That something was *placenta previa*, a condition in which the placenta forms abnormally across the uterus. We learned of it the night of her first hemorrhage, a hemorrhage so severe that we thought she was having a miscarriage. She spent the next two months at total bed rest, because the slightest movement could incite another hemorrhage.

Twice more during those long worrisome weeks a hemorrhage took us back to the hospital. The third time, the doctors said enough was enough. My wife could take no more and the baby would be taken by emergency cesarean.

Because she was already anemic and now hemorrhaging again, Beth's trip to the operating room was like one of those television medical dramas with doctors and nurses racing her gurney down the hospital corridor tying up the loose ends of their gowns as they went. I ran with them, and just before they peeled me off at the O.R. doors, I asked the doctor if the baby was going to be all right. All he said, and rather curtly, was that they were working to save my wife.

Almost two hours later the doctor informed me that she had tolerated the surgery well and that I could see her soon. He said the baby was struggling and was being prepared for transport to another hospital better equipped to meet her pressing needs. A daughter, I had another daughter, who might not survive.

I waited until I saw Beth safely in a room before leaving. She had already been informed of everything and urged me to the other hospital and whatever needed doing for our baby. It was almost 11:00 P.M. in late November. Anxious and afraid, I drove the dark miles between hospitals in a pouring rain. In such moments we experience an otherwise distant clarity, revealing both the amazingly few things that truly matter, and the visceral power these few things possess.

When I reached the other hospital's lobby, I was torn between finding our daughter and going to admitting for the necessary paperwork. Doing as I had been told, I went to admitting. When we were done, a woman there gave me directions to the neonatal intensive care unit.

I had already seen our daughter once, briefly, as doctors and nurses at her birth hospital frantically attached what seemed like dozens of tubes to two pounds of flesh. I had seen her tiny extremities through the gaps that occasionally opened among them as they worked over and around her. I had seen her heaving chest, fighting for every breath. I wasn't sure I could bear to see more. I feared that she might be struggling even more severely, or not struggling at all.

When I arrived at the doors of the unit and announced my presence through an intercom, a doctor soon appeared and explained things to me. Our daughter was now settled in what would be her home for the next two months. Her condition was simple, born too soon and with tiny membrances were tiny lungs should have been. He was a kind man and assured me that she just might make it. He would do his best.

He asked me if I would like to see her and I said no. He seemed surprised, but understanding. The nurse standing behind him wasn't as understanding. "Come in and see your daughter," she said, rather sternly. But I couldn't do it. I told her so and abruptly left, informing her I would be back the following morning. I was afraid my daughter was going to die, and I couldn't believe I could bear getting any more attached.

In order to improve our daughter's chance of survival, my wife pumped breast milk at her hospital every morning. We timed things so that I arrived at the hospital each morning about the time she was finished pumping. I then transported the fresh milk to the baby's hospital. The morning of my first delivery, as a nurse in the neonatal unit took the container of milk from me, she asked if I wanted to come in and see my daughter. "No," I said, "I have to get to work." After work, I visited Beth until the end of visiting hours and went straight home.

The following morning, when I made the milk drop at our daughter's hospital, a different nurse came to the door of the unit. As I handed over the milk, her hand bypassed the proffered parcel grabbing my wrist instead. "Come in," she said. "Come in and see your daughter." It wasn't a gentle grab. She latched onto my wrist with an iron grip. I was going into that unit. I was going to see my daughter.

"Where is she?" I asked as she pulled me in and closed the door firmly behind us. I looked around at a host of nurses, tiny babies in incubators, and medical equipment. The faces of all the nurses told me they were in cahoots. "Go over there and wash up," the iron nurse said in response to my question. "You will want to reach in and touch her."

"I don't want to touch her. I'll just see her."

"Go wash your hands."

Those nurses seemed prepared to move me to the sink and wash my hands for me if I hesitated much longer. I did as I was told.

So there I stood, next to our daughter's incubator. There were still lots of tubes, and she was still breathing hard, but not with the same difficulty as before. She seemed more peaceful. She lay on her back, little arms and legs spread out to both sides with her head facing away from me. The nurse, the iron nurse, bent down next to one of the little holes in the incubator and said in the kindest, sweetest voice, "Katherine, your Daddy's here." And then she stepped back and away. (The nurse was thus the first person to attach the name we had chosen for a girl to the person we had been generically referring to as "the baby.")

It seemed that we were alone now in all the world, Katherine and I. I loved her with all my heart.

"Reach in and touch her," said a voice from behind me. "Go ahead, it's OK."

I bent down and reached my hand through one of the little holes in the side of the incubator. As I did, Katherine turned her head toward me, wrapped the teensy fingers of her tiny hand as far around my index finger as they would go, and smiled.

She smiled!

I heard a collective gasp from the array of nurses hovering behind me. Even they were startled, and as moved and amazed as I. I was overwhelmed by a sense of well-being and hope. I felt surrounded by love. I was not comforting Katherine, she was comforting me. I was being comforted, by my tiny daughter, those nurses, and God.

That night, when visiting with my wife, I related as best I could what had transpired. She shared that she too had felt an overwhelming sense of hope and confidence in Katherine's future all day. She was moved but not really surprised by my story.

I arrived home late to the sound of our phone ringing. It was a friend and coworker who simply wanted me to know that everybody at work was thinking of us and praying for us. I can still hear the hope and strength in his closing words to me that night, words spoken almost thirty years ago: "I just know everything's going to be O.K." "Yes," I replied, "I believe it too."

The next day, Katherine's doctor informed us that literally overnight membranes had become lungs. He was encouraged. Many difficult hurdles lay ahead, but her chances of survival were greatly improved.

God's commanding touch can be so delicate in application, so unlikely in source, so incomprehensible for all its specificity.

Why Misti?

CAROL STIGGER

The chaplain performed the nuptial service before three hundred guests, most of them in tears. "Today, we gather here to witness a miracle," he began.

The mother of the bride, Louise Ray Morningstar, watched her daughter, Misti—dressed in white satin, pearls, and lace—let go of her father's arm and take the hand of her groom. Louise's tears were more than tears of joy—they were tears of hope realized and years of uncertainty swept away.

Mothers of daughters assume, from the moment they know their baby is a girl, that one day that tiny armful of human potential will be a beautiful bride, physically, emotionally, and spiritually equipped to fulfill her destiny as a woman.

For seventeen years, nothing nibbled away at Louise's maternal assumptions. She watched the evening news from a detached distance, with its images of blood and twisted metal, microphones shoved into faces haloed by the neon lights of emergency rooms as if stunned "next of kin" could wrap words around the sudden death of their expectations. Louise knew that tragedy could strike as close as next door, but she never imagined tragedy striking her own children.

Her assumptions grew firmer as Misti bloomed. Her childhood love of rhythm matured into the dedicated study of ballet. Misti applied her genius IQ at a demanding boarding school to gain academic grounding and discipline for medical school and earn the credentials she needed to give back to a world that had given so much to her. Just looking at Misti, the grace of her stride, her beauty, assured Louise that this child was blessed. Nor was Misti's loveliness superficial. Her strong sense of personhood and her dignity quietly commanded respect, while the exuberance of her teenage years brought frequent smiles. She had best friends and good friends, and she knew the difference between them. She edited the yearbook, and she shopped with a passion. She had a boyfriend, Max, and in her closet hung a formal gown purchased months before her senior prom.

All that ended in a moment, beneath an 18-wheeler, where Misti lay crushed in the family car, which she had been driving to the mall. The truck driver walked away unharmed, stammering, "I never saw the intersection." Later, he paid a $40 traffic fine. Misti was taken away by helicopter. While a team of doctors fought to keep her lungs working and her heart beating, a nurse slipped a "Jane Doe" identification bracelet on her arm.

Louise and her husband, Harry, were in the Caribbean celebrating their new direction in life. After thirty-five years of marriage, two sons launched into adulthood, and Misti soon to enter college, they had sold their two businesses and decided to enjoy the good life. They would take trips, spend more time with friends and family, and enjoy the world's beauty in leisure. They watched the sunset over the ocean and had their last carefree conversation for five years.

It was just hours from that sunset to the high-tech life support systems surrounding Misti. In those hours a mother's questions changed from "Where will Misti go to college?" to "Will Misti last the hour?" to "Will she last the night?"

After a month of many close calls with death, Misti's condition stabilized. She was in a coma, diagnosed with "brain trauma." Louise was warned not to expect further improvement in her daughter's quality of life. That day, she noticed a brain trauma patient making a great effort to propel his wheelchair. Inch by inch, the chair moved toward a spot of sun beneath a window. Louise realized that she had no assumptions left, only hope that the daughter who wanted to be a doctor would one day be able to push her wheelchair to a sunny spot. Hope is what kept Louise fighting for every inch of progress that friends and family, doctors and therapists, and she herself could wrestle from her daughter's deep sleep. For a month they walked the tightrope between hope and dread. Now Misti was opening her eyes for short periods of time. Perhaps she was slowly reconnecting with the world, but no one knew what remained of the young woman she had been.

Through months of daylong visits in the rehabilitation hospital, Louise learned that coming out of a coma is not the gentle awakening Hollywood portrays. This is particularly true when the brain has been traumatized and all the circuits broken, bruised, or rearranged as Misti's were. She could sit in a wheelchair, but her muscles had not relearned their functions. Every limb, her torso, and her head had to be propped, strapped, restrained. Before she could learn to speak again, she had to learn to swallow, to move her lips, control her tongue. This seventeen-year-old honor student was in diapers; she wore bibs and she drooled. She made progress in regaining control of her body through intensive therapy and a mother who complained if she did not get every full session that was ordered. Louise learned the techniques and worked with her daughter, giving all the energy she could muster to the task of salvaging all of Misti that could be recovered.

Progress was slow but definite. Misti touched everything to learn how it felt, put everything in her mouth to learn how it tasted. Louise helped her daughter navigate a second infancy, but this time with no expectations of how far she would progress. Only hope remained that having beaten the odds by surviving, Misti would conquer the next hurdle. Louise did not dwell on any thoughts beyond that.

As she regained strength, sweet-natured Misti began behaving like a wild animal. She would be very still, but when anyone got near, she would attack, biting the nearest arm, hand, or leg. The doctor explained that she was fighting to get out of the coma, to make contact in any way possible. During this phase, her grandmother was able to visit her for the first time. She was shocked and grieved. "Why Misti?" she cried. After endless days and nights of her own heart asking "Why Misti?" Louise answered, "Why not Misti? Perhaps God felt we were more able to handle the devastating results of such an accident than some other parents."

Louise steeled herself for the next hurdle, which turned out to be a nightmare. In addition to reconnecting with the world through the use of her teeth, now Misti became an exhibitionist, stripping off her clothes and yelling swear words. The rehab team was pleased at the progress these actions represented. Louise focused on the word "progress" and trusted that her daughter would regain her dignity someday.

Months later, the rehab hospital discharged Misti to her family's care and prescribed a full schedule of physical, mental, and psychological therapy. At that time Misti was functioning intellectually at a fourth-grade level and had the emotional maturity of a three-year-old. Her emotional makeup was seriously damaged. She would laugh instead of cry. She was convinced that events she saw on television happened to her. Her fierce temper tantrums made her nearly impossible to control. Yet, Louise accepted the challenge of taking her daughter home less than a year after the accident. As they left the hospital, she heard a nurse say, "I don't know where that woman gets her guts, but if I ever get hurt, I want her on my side."

It would be four-and-a-half more years before Misti was fully launched back into life.

As a baby, Misti had not entered the strong and capable Morningstar family in the way you may have assumed. This child of the heart—reborn through a family's five years of labor, tears, exhaustion, and pain—was not expected, but selected. Misti had been adopted at ten weeks, although the system was against placing a healthy newborn with parents so near the arbitrary cut-off age who had two birth children of their own. But Misti had a flaw that opened a crack in the system and placed her in Louise's arms: On each little foot, Misti had an extra toe.

From layette to bridal veil, Misti's life journey was not what her mother had imagined. The detour through brain trauma left lasting scars. Misti graduated from college, but medical school was out of the question. Her emotions are unpredictable, and some tasks are difficult. Some may always be impossible. Regression is a possibility, but so is continued progress. Louise knows that lives are built on reality and not on assumptions. Holding Misti's son in her arms and knowing how dearly her son-in-law loves her daughter are miracles as well as the assurance she needs to know that Misti is fulfilling her destiny.

And so is Louise. She chronicled Misti's story in a book, *Journey Through Brain Trauma: A Mother's Story of Her Daughter's Recovery.* And five years after that carefree sunset over the ocean, Louise and her husband began their retirement again. "I'm not the person I was before the accident," she says. "I have a hard time listening to people who take a 'poor me' stance to their lives. At the same time, I make more time for what's really important: my family, beauty, good friends."

A Chance to Forgive

FRANCES MCGEE

Thursday. My turn to pick up doughnuts for the Montgomery County Prosecutor's office where I work. I was in a rush, as usual, but it wouldn't take long to swing by my favorite bakery. It was good to see so much activity on a gray February morning: kids holding their parents' hands as they walked to school, folks hurrying to work. But one man stood out. He was pacing in front of the parking lot next to the bakery, wearing a rumpled overcoat and a blue knit hat. His body language made me wary. As a prosecutor, I'm trained to notice these things. I drove past the lot and pulled up on the street, as close to the bakery as I could get.

I quickly paid for my doughnuts and fished my keys from my pocket. I was heading back to my car when I spotted him again. Probably a crackhead the way he slouched. I picked up my pace. Just then he stepped in front of me.

"This is a robbery," he snarled. "Don't make it difficult."

Did he say he's going to rob me? I'd heard it described

hundreds of times by victims: time seemed to slow and a feeling of unreality set in.

"Hurry up!" he said. He unzipped his coat, revealing an opened switchblade. Yet, I was frozen with shock, a combination of fear, disbelief, and anger. Anger that this could happen to me. He reached out and yanked my purse off my arm in a single, violent motion. My keys and the doughnuts tumbled to the pavement.

The mugger pointed the knife, pushing it at me as a warning. Then he sprinted down the alley and through the parking lot, clutching my bag. I let loose a scream that had been building in the few seconds that the mugging occurred. It curdled my own blood. I trembled uncontrollably. Somehow I made it back to the bakery and used their phone to call my husband.

"I've been robbed," I managed to gasp. "My purse is gone. Wallet. Everything."

"I'll be right there," he said. "All that matters is that you're okay."

He was right, of course. I was lucky not to get hurt. I've said the same thing to victims. But okay? Certainly not. This time I was the victim. I'd been violated.

The police came and found the robber's coat and hat in a search of the area. There were hairs that could be used for a DNA sample. The next day I skipped work to review hundreds of mug shots at the police station, but I couldn't match my assailant's face to a known felon's.

Worse, all those mug shots of all those criminals made me feel vulnerable. I didn't want to be alone. And I felt I could never go back to my favorite little bakery.

I lay in bed that night unable to rest. I should have felt secure beside my husband, but my thoughts were trained on the stranger who'd done this terrible thing. Would he come after me? He knew where I lived now that he had my wallet. I closed my eyes and tried to sleep. Impossible. The anger I felt during the attack welled up and I fantasized that I'd fought back. I felt bolder. I visualized myself standing tall in the courtroom at his sentencing, upbraiding this villain for what he'd done to me. I wanted him to pay.

I awoke in the morning still feeling vengeful. I had a right, though, didn't I? I sat down alone at my dining-room table, sipping my coffee. I felt rage overtaking me, and I didn't like it. I needed to pray. *God, I know you protected me from the mugger's knife. Now protect me from my hateful feelings.* In the stillness of the room, an answer came: *have the church pray for the robber.*

Pray for him? The criminal? That wasn't what I expected. Yet throughout the day the thought kept popping up. Finally I dialed my pastor's number. I was indignant as I told Father Ben what had happened. "Pray for my attacker!" I said. "That's crazy, right?"

"Maybe not," Father Ben said. "Just make sure to come to church tomorrow."

The next morning during the service Father Ben stood in front of the altar. "Please join me, Frances," he said.

The surprise must have been plain on my face. I rose hesitantly and walked down the aisle till I reached his side. "Frances was mugged on Thursday in an act of terrible violence," he announced. There was a collective gasp. "Let us give thanks for her deliverance from harm." Heads bowed and whispered prayers filled the sanctuary. Next, Father Ben asked us all to pray once more. This time, incredibly, for the robber. "Release him from his dependence on drugs, Lord," he said. "Show him your way. The way to you. The way to forgiveness."

"Your way," I repeated. My way was vengeance. I certainly had a right to be upset, even angry. I had a right to demand justice. But I also needed to let it all go, to let God. I closed my eyes and prayed with my whole being. I would not meet evil with evil. Show him the way to forgiveness, I repeated, and laid my fears and anger at the foot of the cross.

When I returned to work on Monday each of my coworkers stopped by to see me. The support felt good, but things weren't right yet. There was one thing I had to conquer.

"I'll bring the doughnuts tomorrow," I announced on Wednesday afternoon. "Thursday's my day."

"Where are you gonna get them?" a colleague asked, furrowing her brow.

"Same place," I said.

Thursday morning. I retraced the steps I'd taken a week earlier. I parked in the same spot, went into the bakery and strode back out minutes later with a box of Dayton's best doughnuts. My coworkers cheered as I carried the box into the office like a trophy. Scared? Yeah, a little bit. I'd learned that there are things out there we need to be scared of, and more so that the Lord protects us from harm not only from others but from our own feelings.

More than a year has passed and my robber hasn't been apprehended. I still ask God to direct his life and deliver him from the forces making him cause pain to others. Of course I still hope he'll be caught. When he is, I hope he'll know he's been given a chance to change. When God gives you a chance, you take it. I know. After all, he gave me one: a chance to forgive.

Ice Cream for My Kids

DEBBIE DAVIS

Do you mind if I buy ice cream cones for your kids?"
"Why . . . no. I don't guess so," I stammered. But
the truth is that I did mind. Of all the people on earth
that I didn't want involved with my two children, this
man topped the list.

I didn't see him often, but for the past nine years,
every time I did cross his path my breath shortened, my
gut knotted, and every fiber within me cried out.

"I don't want an ice cream cone," Eric objected. Eric
was my oldest. He was twelve and perpetually hungry,
especially right now, since we had come straight to the
Dairy Queen that night after his seventh-grade basketball
game. In moments like this I had been noticing signs that
Eric lacked a steadying male hand in his life.

"You gotta be nice and eat it anyway," Erin said,
assuming her proper sister role—as she did too often I
feared—to fill in some of the parenting that was missing.
Her reproving scowl silenced Eric's protests.

At church one Sunday morning about three months
before this—or was it four?—I had spotted that familiar

face in the worshiping crowd, and the very sight of the man as he slipped into a pew across the sanctuary had triggered a spiritual tempest in my soul.

The first Scripture verses I learned as a child in that same church were Jesus's words in "The Lord's Prayer." And you know, of course, that right after the famous prayer comes Christ's promise, "If you forgive others the wrongs they have done to you, your Father in heaven will also forgive you" (Matthew 6:14 TEV).

Remembering those words was bad enough—since my soul was overloaded with hate and hurt and anger toward this man I had just spotted—but Jesus then adds a line that drove a spike into my heart when I recalled it. "If you do not forgive others," he warns, "then your Father will not forgive the wrongs you have done."

Yes, Lord, I answered in my mind. *I know you're talking to me. But how can I possibly forgive that man? You know how much he took away from me. You know what havoc his foolishness wreaked in our lives. Forgive* him?

But even as my quarrel with God blocked out the hymn that had just begun, deep in my heart I knew how wrong I was. For months before that morning in the church I had been slowly facing up to the hard truth that I had no choice but to forgive this man who had wrecked my life. The Lord was helping me to see that my failure to do so would only add to the damage he had done.

On that evening in August 1984 my phone rang. "Greg has been involved in an accident," they told me. "Greg's gone," his brother told me when I got to the hospital. At first I could not hear the truth. I didn't want to hear the truth. "Gone where?" I wanted to know.

When it finally soaked in that Greg was dead, my fairy tale world was obliterated in that instant.

My perfect marriage to the man of my dreams was over, just like that.

The father of my two little ones was gone. Forever. And they were so young—just three years old and eighteen months—they would likely not remember him.

Never again would Greg embrace me. Never again would I see the twinkle in his eyes as he teased me.

On a farm-to-market road east of town Greg had been biking that afternoon. Not just for fun. Greg was training seriously. He thought he had a good shot at competing in the triathlon, so he was pushing himself. During those days he spent lots of time on his bike out on the open roads north of town. He hoped to be in top shape by the time the competition began. In the days right before the accident, he also had been thinking of attempting the Iron Man competition in Hawaii.

I know my head-over-heels love for him probably distorted my estimate, but Greg really was something special. At heart he was a good man, and he was an athlete's athlete—lean, trim, hard as rock, with stamina that made me marvel. His triathlon dreams were my dreams as well. Together we were going for the gold.

All of that ended so senselessly, so suddenly. Three or four beers too many turned a neighbor's ancient dump truck into a high-speed killing machine. My dear Greg never knew what hit him. The stats that day were really quite simple. One drunk driver equaled one dead man. My man.

After Greg left our house that afternoon, I never saw him again. Not even at the funeral home or in the coffin at the service at the church. When the truck smashed into him, Greg's body had been so mutilated and mangled that the seasoned lawmen who came to the scene were undone. Normally as the wife of the victim I would have been required to identify Greg's body, but the coroner took one look at what remained of his torso and said no.

In the dark, muddled days after the accident, I was consumed with rage at the very idea that anybody could be so mindless, so careless of others. I didn't plot specific revenge, but with my whole being I wished for some dread disaster to befall the wretch who had destroyed my family and ruined our lives. When the legal system turned the dump truck driver loose unpunished, my seething outrage boiled over.

Blinded by my own anguish, I had given no thought to how the guilt of the man's offense might be troubling his heart. In fact, it was hard for me to imagine that he had a heart. Self-pity had duped me into demonizing the man. To me he was no longer Mr. Smith or Mr. Jones who lived in the gray house past the Coop Gin. In my grief-tormented mind he had become Greg's killer, and although the courts decided otherwise, I was consumed by the conviction that he deserved to pay for his sins.

Looking back now, I can see that the poor fellow must have been devastated by what he had done. More than once through mutual acquaintances he inquired, "Can I come apologize to you and your kids?" Once at church he literally fell at my feet and begged for my forgiveness. But I wanted no part of it at the time.

Years ago my former pastor, Dr. Doug Manning, wrote a best-selling little book which he titled, *Don't Take My Grief Away from Me!* That's how I felt. That book was about me. Every time the man who killed Greg tried to make things right, I rebuffed him. In my heart I screamed, "Don't try to take my wounds, my hurt, my bitterness away from me!"

That day in church just months before the Dairy Queen encounter, however, the Lord finally got through to me. I left worship that morning with a new conviction that I had to find some way to turn loose of the hate that festered in my soul. I knew I needed to. Of that much I now was convinced. But I had no idea how to go about it.

Then, out of the blue, just a few weeks later here came that awful man across the Dairy Queen wanting to buy ice cream for my kids. "Okay, Lord," I surrendered, although it violated everything carnal in my soul. Stifling the long-rehearsed anger that welled up inside me, I looked at the man and forced my head to nod yes.

When the ice cream was gone, I hustled my brood into our aging Tahoe despite their varying complaints. "But I wanted a triple hamburger," Eric fussed. The ice cream cone had not satisfied his hunger.

But Erin, wise beyond her ten years, ignored her brother's protests and asked me, "Who was that guy, Mom? And why did he want to buy us ice cream?"

When I told the kids who the man was and what he had done, they were quiet for the longest time. We drove home in silence as I pondered the spiritual chasm the Lord has just helped us to cross.

Nothing to Hide

DEB SISTARE

I was fifteen when my dad died, and Mom took our family to live with Grandma and Grandpa. They were a perfect pair of opposites. She was short and plump; he was tall and skinny. She had a head full of wild white hair; he had a thin band of fuzz from ear to ear. She was always in high gear; he walked with an easy shuffle. Grandma went to church on Sundays; Grandpa didn't.

"Why doesn't Grandpa go with us?" I finally asked my mother one Sunday while we were getting ready.

"He just doesn't," Mom said. "And you shouldn't ask such personal questions of people. It's just not polite."

I hadn't meant to be hurtful. I loved Grandpa. After school I'd stop off at his barbershop and watch him cut hair in his careful, deliberate way. On warm summer evenings we'd sit under the pecan tree, and Grandpa would teach me life lessons.

"If you borrow money and say you'll pay it back Friday morning, then do it," he said. "Even if you have to borrow it again on Friday night."

Some nights, when Grandpa fell asleep in his old

lounge chair, I'd put on red lipstick and kiss him on his bald head. When he woke up and came into the kitchen, Grandma would burst out laughing.

"What's so funny?" Grandpa would ask, two red lips standing out on his shiny head. Then he'd see me struggling to keep a straight face and go to the mirror, knowing I'd gotten him again.

Much as I became Grandpa's shadow, though, some things remained a mystery. Like why did Grandpa smell of cherry pipe tobacco during the week and on the weekends smell like whiskey? Plus, I'd seen his name on the church roll. Why had he stopped going?

One weekend I found Grandma frantically pulling towels out of the closet in the bathroom.

"Did you lose something?" I asked.

Grandma shook her head and stuffed a few more towels under her arm. "There it is," she said, sounding relieved. She held an unmarked bottle of amber liquid I knew was whiskey. As I watched, Grandma poured a trickle down the drain of the chipped porcelain sink. "If I empty it he'll just buy another bottle," she explained as she added water. "So I dilute it a little at a time. By tomorrow he'll be sober enough to go to work." Grandma put the bottle back in the closet. "I can't let him lose the barbershop."

Without asking any questions, I handed her the towels, one by one, until everything was back in its place.

I watched Grandpa closely that week, but didn't

notice anything unusual until Friday night. I smelled whiskey on him. When we got back from church on Sunday afternoon he was dozing in his easy chair. *He doesn't look drunk,* I thought. But when he got up and walked past me, eyes downcast, he didn't smile. His feet dragged like lead weights across the floor and into the bathroom.

I went to find my mother. She was reading in her bedroom. "What is it, Deb?" Mom asked. I hesitated.

"Is Grandpa okay?" I managed finally.

"Sure," Mom said, her tone clipped. "He's just tired. He worked hard all week." She went back to her book. *Grandpa's just tired,* I repeated to myself. Then I heard Grandma wrestling with the towels in the bathroom closet and went to help her. She stacked them in my outstretched arms. Grandpa must have been ashamed of his drinking, I figured, and that's why he tried to hide it from Grandma. Maybe that's why he doesn't go to church anymore. He wants to hide from God. Like the week before, Grandma stuck the bottle under the faucet without a word.

After a while our Sunday routine seemed almost normal. Almost. Grandpa remained the same loving man, and he continued to be "tired" on the weekends. I grew up and moved out on my own, but I still visited my family regularly.

When I was 30, Grandpa was diagnosed with terminal cancer. I spent a lot of time sitting beside his bed, talking to him. The whiskey bottle was never far away now. *He's too sick to hide it anymore,* I thought one night as I watched him sleep. Grandpa had spent too much of his life trying to keep his problem from us and from God. The worst part was that we had helped him do it.

"You should have asked God for help," I whispered to Grandpa, kissing his bald head. "We all should have."

Then I had an awful thought: *if Grandpa's secret had kept him from church, could it keep him out of heaven as well? Please, God, forgive us all. And take my grandpa into heaven.*

After Grandpa died, the thought continued to haunt me. One night I had a strange dream. Grandpa was standing at the bottom of a steep, pearl-white staircase that reached way into the clouds. He gazed up at a huge angel, who held out a satiny, emerald-colored robe, open and waiting, it seemed, for Grandpa himself. When Grandpa headed up the stairs, he wasn't shuffling. At the top of the stairs, the angel helped Grandpa into the robe and tied the sash so the rich folds of material fell around him. Then the angel took Grandpa's hand, and together they disappeared into the clouds.

The picture of Grandpa wrapped in that shiny emerald-green robe was fresh in my mind when I met Grandma for lunch the next day.

Grandma was adjusting slowly to life without Grandpa. "I miss him terribly," she admitted. "He was a good man. Even though he had a drinking problem."

I couldn't believe she had said it openly.

"Yes," I said, "he did have a drinking problem." It was a relief to admit it aloud. But Grandma looked frightened.

"He didn't go to church," she said. "I don't know if he asked God's forgiveness. I'm so afraid he didn't go to heaven!"

I wrapped my arms around Grandma, feeling closer to her than I ever had in all the years I'd lived in her house. The secret that had always stood between us was gone.

"Last night I dreamed about Grandpa," I said. Grandma sat very still and listened. When I got to the part where Grandpa slipped into the green robe, her eyes filled with tears. "He made it, Deb," she said. "He really made it."

"But, Grandma, it was just a dream."

Grandma shook her head. "Let me tell you something," she said. An expression came over her face that I'd never seen before. "Something we never told anybody else. One Sunday at church when we were first married, your grandpa saw an angel standing right on the altar. He said that angel was at least ten feet tall, standing right behind the preacher and smiling down at him during the service. And your grandpa said that angel was wearing the most beautiful green robe—'a robe that glistened like emeralds' were the words he used. 'When I get to heaven,' he said, 'I want a green robe just like the one that angel was wearing.' What else could that dream be but a sign from God that Grandpa is with him?"

What else, indeed. God sees our weaknesses, and he loves us despite them. I believe he has an angel with an emerald-green robe waiting to welcome each of us, flaws and all.

Chapter 2

Reclaiming Hearts

I will praise you, LORD, with all my heart. I will tell all the miracles you have done (Psalm 9:1 NCV).

People often suffer from wounded hearts, whether wounded on purpose or unknowingly. And the only way to reclaim a heart that has been injured is through forgiveness. The wounded person forgives the offenders, even if the offenders don't ask for that forgiveness or know they need to ask. Forgiveness, you see, should be freely given just as we freely received it from the One who forgave us when we were so unforgivable.

Lost and Found

B. J. TAYLOR

It was a perfect summer day, hot and sunny and just right for a swim.

We'd been waiting all morning for the guys to get to the lake. They finally pulled up in Tom's car. He had his best friend John with him, but Tom always drove when we did anything as a foursome. Cathy liked that. There were lots of things she liked about him, and he liked her too. They were even talking about getting married.

The two guys did everything together. When Tom and Cathy hooked up, John started dating me, Cathy's little sister. "Hey, what took you guys so long?" Cathy asked playfully as Tom walked up and gave her a warm hug.

"It was hard to find this place," Tom answered.

Suddenly, John yelled, "Let's go get wet!"

The four of us ran down the path leading from the parking lot to the lake below. We reached the sand, tossed off our shoes, and looked out at the water. It was a shimmery blue and as calm as the day. Not a ripple on the surface or a cloud in the sky.

"Last one to the raft is a rotten egg!" Tom shouted.

He raced into the water and began to swim toward the wooden raft anchored a ways from shore.

Cathy was the first to get there, and I climbed up right after. John soon joined us. "Where's Tom?" he asked.

"Oh, he's such a prankster, he's probably hiding behind the raft," Cathy said. We looked, but he wasn't there. We scanned the water and the shoreline, but didn't see any sign of him. "Tom!" we called out again and again. "Tom, where are you?" We swam back to shore, but couldn't find him anywhere.

By the time divers found Tom at the bottom of the lake, the victim of a strong undercurrent, it was too late. Mom and Dad tried to calm Cathy, but she ran to the end of the beach, screaming. I watched the divers put his body in a black bag with a long zipper. They placed him on a stretcher and carried it up the hill. Tom was gone at the age of twenty.

Someone found Tom's personal items at the edge of the beach where he'd left them. They put his watch into Cathy's hands along with his comb from his back pocket. Later that day Dad drove Cathy over to Tom's house. They had to tell his family. His brother wanted Tom's watch so she gave it to him. But she kept the comb. She said it smelled like his hair.

I'd never been to a funeral before. There was a cross with a figure of crucified Jesus near Tom's casket. I didn't think about my faith much. It was just there. Like the sunrise in the morning, I never questioned it. I always thought God would protect me, and those I loved. But now I felt that protection slip away. Where were you, God, when Tom needed you?

Time passed slowly. John and I invited Cathy to the movies, and to restaurants, but it was three of us instead of four. It wasn't the same.

Eventually, Cathy met a man she admired. He loved fishing and motorcycle riding. His name was Mark. They had fun together and he made her laugh. She asked John and me to be part of their wedding party, and we gladly accepted. Cathy and Mark set up a small apartment and soon after she added a son. She'd always wanted to take Bible study classes and looked forward to doing that now that they were settled. I thought they'd live happily ever after. That's the way it's supposed to go, right? Only it didn't.

Mark was a big fan of bass fishing. He was invited to go out on a boat in the Wisconsin River with friends for the weekend. He couldn't wait to bring home his catch. "I'll see you Sunday night," he said when he kissed Cathy and their son good-bye. He grinned as he trudged out the door with poles and overnight gear.

Sunday afternoon a car pulled up behind the apartment. It was Mark's mom. "There's been a terrible accident," she said between sobs. "Their boat went over a spillway in the river. Mark didn't make it to shore."

"I feel sure he's still alive," Cathy said. "Maybe he's just unconscious or can't find his way."

The authorities dredged the deep and fast-running river with grappling hooks, trying to locate Mark's body. Cathy held onto her hope as one long day turned into the next. She prayed to God that Mark would come back to her.

But the next weekend he was found. He'd been in the water more than seven days. Shaking, she called our dad with the news. "It happened again," she said sobbing through her tears. "Why, Dad? Why me?"

There was another funeral. Her second. With her baby on her hip, she caressed the closed casket. Cathy couldn't even see her husband one last time. I noticed a cross. Another cross, just like the one at Tom's funeral. I closed my eyes and screamed inside my head. *God, where were You? Cathy and her baby need Mark. Couldn't You have helped him?*

But there were no answers.

She was on her own.

"I've got to get away," she told me one night. Cathy packed up their clothes and drove down to Florida. She had family there to stay with.

"Come on over for pizza tonight," a friend of the family said one afternoon a few weeks after she'd arrived. "Everyone is welcome."

She walked in with her son in tow. He was a rambunctious almost two-year-old and into everything. And he loved pizza.

"Hi, Cathy, glad you and your boy could make it," the host said. "Help yourself, we've got plenty." She looked at the five large pizza boxes on the dining room table. They held everything from plain cheese to one loaded with sausage, pepperoni, green peppers, mushrooms, onions, and black olives.

"That one is my favorite," said a voice behind her.

She turned around. Towering above her five-foot-four-inch frame was a mammoth man. Well over six feet tall, he had longish brown hair and a captivating smile.

"Is this your boy?" He picked up Timmy with ease. "He's cute," he said as he tousled her son's red hair. After putting him back down, he grabbed a couple of plates and loaded up. "See ya later," he said.

The next couple of months Cathy ran into him quite often. They were often invited to the same places and enjoyed long discussions about anything and everything. She found herself thinking about him even when they weren't together. But her fear stopped her from pondering a future with him. One night she prayed, *God, every time I love someone You take him from me. How am I supposed to trust that it won't happen again?*

With a young son, life was a constant job of cleaning and picking up. But they often went to the park and got down and dirty in the sandbox racing Matchbox cars. Or they climbed the slide over and over for that thrill of a swift ride to the bottom, landing smack dab in the sand. So with a huge basket straddling her hip she walked into the laundromat with their dirty clothes one day. Timmy found a table and pulled out his crayons and coloring book, and Cathy loaded three washers with their jeans, T-shirts, socks, and underwear. She was just settling into a chair when a woman walked in. Cathy had never seen her before, and she didn't have any clothes to wash or dry. *I wonder what she's looking for?* Cathy thought.

The woman walked straight up to her. "I'd like you to have this," she said. And she handed Cathy a leather-covered Bible. "I go to Bible study classes every week. Would you like to come?"

It had been a while since she'd thought about those classes that she wanted to take when she and Mark were together. Was it time now to let go of her anger and get on with her life?

"You'll find the answers you are searching for," the woman continued.

"I'd love to come to Bible study classes," Cathy found herself saying. She hugged the Bible to her chest as the woman turned and left.

Cathy attended classes for a long time. And she found the answers she craved. It wasn't God's fault that Tom and Mark were taken from her. They were terrible accidents that ended tragically. She studied the Bible long and hard and discovered that God had been holding her in His arms through each funeral, through each day she cried buckets of tears. Even when she didn't trust Him, He was there for her. *I'm sorry, God. I didn't mean to blame You. Please forgive me,* she cried out in anguish one day.

Her burdens finally lifted when she forgave God and also herself. She was ready to begin her new life, and it included the wonderful, towering man. He adopted her son, Timmy, and they added three more boys to their family. They have been married now more than thirty years. They still order pizza with everything on it. It's become Cathy's favorite too.

Fussing, Fighting, and Forgiving

PHILIP GULLEY

A friend of mine was fired from his job a while back. He came to tell me about it. He was embarrassed and didn't want to use the word "fired," but that's what had happened. He'd made his boss mad and had been fired. He was discouraged. I told him not to worry about it, that people get fired all the time and go on to better things.

I was fired from the first church I ever pastored. I had been there three months when an elderly woman asked a theological question about the end times. I told her my honest opinion, which must have been the wrong thing to do, because the next Sunday they held a meeting to talk about firing me. They told me if I changed my mind, I could keep my job. I asked them why they would want a pastor who surrendered his convictions just to keep his job. I started to resign but wasn't quick enough, and they fired me.

That very afternoon I got a phone call from another

church to be their pastor. The next Sunday I went to preach a trial sermon. I didn't want to be their pastor because they were a fundamentalist church, and I didn't want to get fired again when they found out what I thought about the end times. So I preached a liberal sermon in hopes they wouldn't hire me. The congregation sat in the pews and squirmed. Except for one dear, sweet, elderly woman who smiled broadly and said, "Amen!" I found out later she was hard of hearing.

After worship they tromped downstairs to talk about whether they should hire me. I sat upstairs in the meeting room and listened through the heating vent. Their initial comments were not promising. I was grateful my mother wasn't there to hear what they were saying about me. But then someone mentioned how maybe God had sent me their way so I could learn a little something. They quieted down and thought about that for a while. Then a man named Dick said, "I think we ought to hire him." Dick had moved to the country after his retirement. He was a big man who brooked no nonsense.

A few minutes later, I heard Dick tramp up the stairs. He sat down on the pew beside me. "We've reached agreement," he reported. "We've also agreed to call you to be our pastor."

I went out to the car, where my wife was waiting. "How did it go?" she asked me.

"Bad news," I told her. "They hired me."

That afternoon the phone rang. It was Dick, asking me if I would play golf with him. I was a little put out with him since he had criticized my sermon. I figured I could pay him back by thrashing him in a game of golf. We met the next morning at the golf course and played nine holes. Dick beat me by ten strokes. Afterward, when he was loading my clubs into the trunk of his car, he shook his head and laughed, "A preacher who can't preach or golf. What have we gotten ourselves into?"

Then he took me back to his house for lunch. I met his wife, Katie, a tender, considerate woman. "Heard about your sermon," she said. She was too polite to tell me what she'd heard about it.

Dick and I became fast friends. When I preached a sermon he didn't like, I was always the first to know. We golfed once a month. I never beat him. Then his elderly mother died, and I conducted her funeral. It was about then that Dick started liking my sermons. I never did figure out if it was because I was changing or because Dick was.

I stayed in that little church for four years. When I left, they gave me a book full of letters about what I meant to them. I sat downstairs in the meetinghouse basement and read it and cried. Wonderful, wonderful, wonderful people.

The next year I was at the hospital, visiting someone

in my new church. I saw Dick walking down the hall. He
was crying. His Katie had died. Dick asked me if I could
give her a funeral, just as I'd said words over his mother.
I have a rule about not going back to a former church to
do funerals or weddings, but I couldn't bring myself to
tell Dick no. Five years before, he'd taken a chance on
me, and I figured that put me in his debt.

A couple of years later, I got a phone call from a lady
in my old church. She told me Dick had cancer. By then
I had children and a busier life. I went by to see Dick
once, but he wasn't there. He died a few months later,
before I could see him again to tell him how much he'd
meant to me. His sons asked me to conduct his funeral.
I broke my rule again and agreed to do it.

At the funeral I talked with some folks about how
Christians these days can't seem to get along. How we
fuss and fight and draw our theological lines in the
sand. I told them how Dick and I were poles apart sometimes, but we'd made up our minds that disagreeing
about God would never keep us from loving God's children. It's good to know where you stand, but it's even
better to have your heart turned toward gentleness.

Dick ended up changing me in ways I needed to be
changed. I'd like to think I did the same for him. Maybe
that's what God has in mind when he brings different
folks together—that we each bring our scraps of truth

and piece them together into this radiant quilt that is so much finer than anything we could have ever made alone.

If I hadn't been fired, I might never have learned that.

If You Only Knew
My Father

LEILANI SHAPLEY

He was an old man who seemed alone in the world. I was a young woman no longer in touch with her father. It's not surprising that we were drawn to each other.

We met the day I started volunteer training at a local convalescent center. Coming up the steps, I saw a big man with thick gray hair sitting in a wheelchair on the porch. He was wearing a bright orange shirt and rainbow-striped suspenders. As I approached the glass doors, he rolled his chair over and struggled forward to grasp the door handle. Then, gallantly holding the door open, he smiled at me. "Name's Ray," he told me in a soft Southern drawl.

"I'm Lani—I'm a new volunteer." I noticed that the thickness of Ray's glasses didn't hide the brightness of his eyes.

"Well, you'll be Bubba to me," he said. "Where I

come from that's a love-name folks give to the little one in the family."

"I like that," I said, and meant it. His way with me was so warm and open, so unlike the gruff indifference my father had always shown me.

Every Wednesday, when I came for training, Ray was waiting at the top of the steps to open the door for me. The volunteers' classes were taught by Sharon, an energetic woman who combined sympathy and faith with a keen understanding of the social and emotional needs of the elderly. When the training was over, the patients I was assigned to didn't include Ray. But I'd visit him on my own time.

His greeting was always an eager, "Hi, Bubba!" Little by little, we stored up facts about each other. When I described my husband to Ray, he told me he was married too. What he said was, "We decided not to get a divorce."

"Do you have any children?"

"Oh, sure."

"Are they able to come visit you?" I asked.

"Oh, yes, they come," he said and looked away. I had never seen anyone visit Ray. *Probably his family lives far away and they don't get here often.*

We spent some time together each week. I bought Ray vitamin C after I read that it might be good for asthma, with which he suffered. I gave him little gifts like a soft beige washcloth and towel. He taught me to play dominoes and saved his dessert for me. With little acts of caring and relaxed conversation, we nourished our relationship.

We grew so close that as I was leaving one day a housekeeper noticed Ray waving to me from the porch and remarked, "Your father sure loves you."

"He's not . . . " My throat closed before I could finish the sentence. I rushed to my car. If you only knew my father! There were no dominoes or desserts from my always too-busy, too-tired father. Most of the time I tried not to think about him because it hurt. But the housekeeper's comment opened up memories.

As usual I went back to the terrible thing he'd done to me on the day of my wedding, the final, embarrassing blow at my reception. The band had begun a waltz and the leader came up to the microphone. "Time for the bride and her father to dance," he announced.

Everyone watched expectantly. "No!" my father said. He turned and left the room, leaving me standing by myself on the dance floor.

When my father turned away from me that day, the bitterness I'd accumulated while I was growing up took over my feelings: all the resentment about his not being on hand for school events, the times he'd threatened to walk away from the burdens of his work and leave my mother and me. I could walk away from him this time. And I did.

That had been five years ago. Once in a while, I thought about trying to patch things up, but it seemed too awkward and complicated. Anyway, I had Ray now.

One day I drove up to the center and Ray wasn't on the porch. I parked the car crookedly and ran up the steps, tripping at the top. Where is he?

I raced to his room. It was empty. No wheelchair, no one in the neatly made bed. "Please, God," I whispered as I backed out of the room. I ran to the nurses' station.

"Where's Ray?" I asked.

"They took him to the hospital last night. His asthma got much worse."

"What hospital?"

"I'll check," the nurse said, going over her charts. "Are you family?"

"I'm his . . . friend." I bit my lip. I'd almost said "daughter."

She gave me the hospital's name.

The trip to the hospital took forever. There I found Ray's room and jolted to a stop in the doorway. His pajama top was off, and he had so many tubes in him. He looked hot and uncomfortable. He turned his head and saw me. "Bubba, I knew you'd find me."

"Ray, you weren't there! I was so scared." I started sobbing.

"Come here, Bubba. It's okay." He held out his arms as best he could. I sat down beside him on the bed and rested my head on his massive chest. Somehow he got an arm around me.

"It's okay, Bubba, you came," he said. "You came to see me." He patted my back. I listened while he talked, and I grew calm.

When it was time to leave, I said, "I'll come to see you tomorrow, Ray."

"Okay, Bubba," he answered.

The next morning I was eating breakfast when the phone rang. I stood to answer it. When I heard Sharon's voice, my hand tightened on the receiver and I leaned against the wall, knocking down the calendar.

"We don't usually do this, but I didn't want you to read it in the paper. I know how close you and Ray were. He died yesterday," she said gently.

"That can't be!" I cried. "I was with him yesterday."

"I know, Lani. He died a few hours later."

After we hung up, I walked slowly outside to the curb and picked up the paper. I turned to the obituaries and read about Ray O'Brien. Suddenly I felt a surge of anger rip through the sorrow. He did indeed have a wife and children! He had 12 children—six sons and six daughters—and all but two of his family lived in the area! And yet I had been the last person to be with him, to comfort him.

I called Sharon back. "Tell me why," I demanded. "Why wasn't his family with him? Why was I the only one with him?"

Sharon hesitated. Finally she began talking. "I'm going to tell you something. I think you deserve to know. Ray was an alcoholic. He beat his wife and his children. When he came to live here, they never wanted to see him again."

"No, I don't believe it," I shouted. Yet I remembered Ray's reluctance to talk about his family. The family who never visited. But this person Sharon was describing couldn't be the loving man who called me Bubba.

"It's true," Sharon said. "But other things are true as well. When he came to the center, Ray talked some things out with me. By then he'd faced the unpleasant facts about himself. He'd been abused as a child, and he realized that one of the reasons he drank was that he thought it helped him with his bad feelings about himself. But it only aggravated them, and then he'd take his anger out on his own family. Over and over he asked God's forgiveness, and he wanted to ask his family to forgive him also. But it was too late. They wanted no part of him."

"I thought of him like a father," I said shakily.

"And Ray thought of you as a daughter. He told me so. You gave him a chance to feel forgiven. It's probably the most Christ-like thing that one person can do for another. I think God used you to comfort a sad, lonely old man with nothing in his life but regrets."

We said good-bye. My thoughts moved slowly, leadenly. Ray and his children were estranged, just as my father and I were. What was it that happened between parents and children? Why were the most damaging relationships so often between those who had the most intimate link—of flesh and blood?

I picked up the calendar I'd knocked off the wall. It was open to June, to a picture of a little girl and her father going fishing. Once, long ago, my father had taken me fishing. It was a good memory, a memory I'd shoved under all the bad ones. It was easier to be mad at my father if I didn't think about the good things—or about the hard life he'd had.

His mother died when he was a small boy, and he'd spent his childhood working in the fields with his father. He'd never gone to high school and had to support my mother and me doing jobs he hated—hauling trash, cleaning the beer coils in bars. Later he built his own business—often working all night and falling into an exhausted sleep in the afternoon. He had done that so I could go to college. "So you don't turn out like me," he often said when I asked why he had to work all the time.

Eventually, as I wandered back in memory, I came to that final, painful incident at my wedding. Then, and only then, did I remember an excuse someone had made for him—one that I had been too hurt to pay attention to. That day my father was wearing his first tuxedo. The fancy clothes—the customs that went with the better life he'd slaved for—were foreign to him. And he didn't know how to dance.

Slowly, I put the calendar back on the wall. Then I picked up the phone. I needed to call my father.

What Happened?

NAOMI LEDERACH

Waking from the fog of anesthesia, Naomi Lederach faintly heard the impersonal words of the nurse beside her: "This bilateral mastectomy is ready to go back to her room." The sentence dug into her hazy brain as Lederach, a nurse herself, struggled to understand what was happening. She sat upright on the gurney and shouted, "That's not me! I just had one breast reconstructed!" The room filled with silence.

She was aware enough to sit up again and look at her chest—it was completely flat. Neither breast was left. Lederach turned to the nurses, yelling, "That's not me! What happened?" She received no answers and slowly slipped back into the fogginess.

Over the next days in recovery, her nightmare continued. "When I came back to the room and really began to face what had happened, I was devastated," she remembers. None of the nursing staff would talk to her about the operation. Fearing a lawsuit, they refused to tell her even the simplest information about her blood pressure or medications.

The doctor was even less help. Whenever he saw her, he was followed by an entourage of residents and interns, and said nothing about her procedure. Not wanting to put him down in front of his students, Lederach found it impossible to broach the subject.

Over the years, Lederach had had five breast biopsies. With the discovery of a sixth lump, and knowing her family's strong history of breast cancer, Lederach's physician recommended a subcutaneous mastectomy. She read up on the procedure in professional journals and involved her husband in the deliberations. They visited with the surgeon—a very professional man who came highly recommended and carefully described exactly what would be done. After months of mulling the decision over, and with the new lump very apparent, they decided to go ahead with the operation—on her right breast. She had never had problems with the left.

Three months after the operation, after the healing process was complete and all the stitches were out, Lederach had her last appointment with the surgeon. She was finally able to ask him what she had so desperately needed to know all along: why?

She asked if it was some sort of miscommunication, or whether he had planned this. "Did he have any idea how it felt to be in that hospital, under his care, feeling as though he had no feeling at all for what had happened?"

The physician still refused to acknowledge that an

error was made. "I think he was very afraid, of course," Lederach said. She reminded him of his order that no medical personnel should talk to her about the operation.

"Well, that's the legal advice we get," he responded.

"Why are you getting legal advice about this if nothing is wrong?" she countered.

He became very defensive and angry. "Well, I can see you haven't worked through this. I will recommend a psychiatrist. I'll write up a referral for you."

"I see psychiatrists every day. I work with them, they are my good friends, and they have helped me to deal with this. And all I'm asking from you is, what happened?"

"I naively thought we could have some sort of resolution to this, in a way that would satisfy," she remembers, "and there was just no way that was going to happen." She became so distraught that she began crying, got down off the table and went to her car. As she drove out on the freeway, Lederach "screamed and cried and poured out my anger and hostility and the devastating feelings I had, all the way home."

Over the next two years, she thought about what she should do about the situation and got a lot of different advice. "People would say, 'You owe it to the public to sue this man so that he doesn't do it again.' Others, of course, from my historical peace church tradition said, 'You really can't sue; you're not supposed to sue your brother.'"

Lederach was very angry with the doctor and making

this decision was extremely difficult. She consulted lawyers to find out what a lawsuit might mean. They assured her she would probably be awarded a large settlement. That knowledge gave Lederach a different kind of feeling, a sense of power—a temptation to hurt the man who had caused her so much pain. "When someone comes to you and is vulnerable and says, 'Will you forgive me?' then it's not so hard to offer forgiveness. [But] where there is a refusal to admit that anything might have been done wrong and forgive anyway, can I do that?"

After eventually making the choice not to sue, Lederach learned that forgiveness is a long process. "I consciously chose, and choose, to forgive him, whether he wants to be forgiven or not. There are times that it comes up, and I get all angry again. And so I chose to reinterpret that history through forgiveness. Not to forgive ties you to the past. And I don't want to be there. I want to move on beyond that."

A Scrapbook of Forgiveness

DARLENE FRANKLIN

My daughter Jolene smiled at me from the photo album. The black-checkered jumper and red beret transformed her into a Parisian school girl. My hand hovered over it, unwilling to make the sacrifice we had agreed upon.

"It's one of my favorites. I hate to give it away." I spoke as much to myself as to my teenage daughter, who was sitting beside me on the couch.

She heard the pleading in my voice but refused to let me back out.

"You said you wanted to give until it hurt. Go ahead and take it out."

The picture joined the pile growing between us. We were going through twenty years of photographs for a very special present: a Christmas gift for my ex-husband, Jolene's father.

Eight years had passed since divorce followed the

discovery that he was abusing our children. Forgiveness did not come easily. At times I burned with anger. Social Services had intervened in our situation, and we fought out custody battles in the courts. The abuse worsened Jolene's already fragile mental state, pushing her over the edge into Post Traumatic Stress Disorder. Our son couldn't decide who to believe, and his behavior worsened when he reached his teen years. I didn't want to forgive the man who refused to admit his misdeeds.

Shortly after the divorce, I discovered the challenge to pray for my former husband. "Love your enemies and pray for those who persecute you, that you may be sons of your Father in heaven" (Matthew 5:44b–45 NIV). After I got used to the idea, it wasn't so bad. Because I wanted the best for our children, I could pray for him. I asked that he would confess his sin. I asked for healing from his past, to free him to be the father our children needed. Even financial blessings: he couldn't pay child support if he didn't make money. I still pray for him on a regular basis.

Along the way my initial anger faded. I no longer wanted to throw him in jail; Jesus's death satisfied any desire I felt for revenge. As my life moved forward, and he remained stuck in place, going through two more failed marriages, the strongest emotion I felt was pity. I thought I had reached the end of the road to forgiveness.

But Jesus's words wouldn't let me alone.

Prayer alone isn't enough.

God? Is that You? What else do You want from me?
Love him.
Love the man who hurt my children so badly?
Love your enemy. For your sake, as much as for his.

I didn't feel love, but I knew that love is a choice. I could show a love I didn't quite feel. My actions could mirror in a small way the sacrificial love God has for me.

And so the family scrapbook project was born. I had kept all of the family pictures when we divorced; it was time to give some back.

I discussed my idea with the only child still at home, Jolene. She agreed to help. I hoped that the gift would help her forgive her father as well. When we opened her baby album, Jolene chose my favorite pictures to send. "I want to give him the best that we have."

Her generosity shouldn't have surprised me (this girl gave her mittens to cold strangers at the bus stop), but it did. Maybe she was more ready to forgive her father than I was. Again I felt God's still, small voice urging me forward. We decided to set aside the best one or two photos from every page of every album.

It took hours to look through everything. Going through pictures from our courtship through our children's early years to the later years apart, I could remember the good times . . . and grieve for the losses.

We filled one large album with photos, wrapped it in bright Christmas paper, and sent it away. I hoped for a positive response. It didn't come. Instead, my ex worried that I hadn't kept pictures of his family for the children. It didn't matter. The last of the lingering bitterness and pain left my heart with the gift.

Unexpected Forgiveness

PAMELA R. WATTS

They were never expecting life to look this way. Surely it was a little too early to have already three divorces between them but perhaps almost too late to be expecting a fresh start with a brand new family. After years of contending with an absentee dad and raising her son, Andrew, as a single mom, Sandra wasn't necessarily anticipating that she would someday find a godly man not only as a partner for her, but also as a role model for her son. While she certainly knew how to pray for such a thing, there was no way she could forecast how this prayer might be answered.

Brian, for his part, did not really expect to see himself as surrogate father to a young boy. Given that he had never really had any deep desire to have children of his own, no one ever expected to see him so excited at the prospect. Perhaps he was surprised to discover the joys of parenthood when viewed through the eyes of a loving and devoted mother like Sandra. When they met through the church singles fellowship, it seemed almost too much to hope for to finally find their soul mates.

Having experienced all too well the pain of divorce, Brian and Sandra were understandably cautious about making any bold declarations or serious plans for their future. Without a doubt there was nothing impulsive or sudden in their courtship as they took measured steps toward a deeper relationship. However, as family and friends observed them together, so certain were we all of an imminent engagement that the only remaining element of surprise came from learning the particulars of how and when Brian would propose. As we eagerly anticipated this joyful event, no one ever could have anticipated what was to come next.

A young man involved in a hit-and-run accident fled the scene only to cause another, and collided with the car carrying Andrew. Andrew was killed instantly, along with another passenger. My husband and I, along with all our extended family, were completely devastated. Having just celebrated the arrival of my first child, when initially I heard the awful news I held my infant daughter in my arms and wept inconsolably for this mother and the child she had just lost.

As the court trial approached, we looked forward to experiencing a measure of relief and the closure that is supposed to come when justice is administered and some kind of restitution exacted. We were not anticipating having to sit through the ordeal of two trials because the first one resulted in a hung jury. We were expecting additionally the jury to be impartial, not indifferent, which seemed the best way to characterize them after they chose to acquit Andrew's killer. As if that were not bad enough, we heard later the appalling news that the defense lawyer flaunted this case as his "proudest victory." In the midst of our bewilderment, anger, and feelings of betrayal, only Sandra remained surprisingly at peace. It was as if she had absolute confidence in God's sure and perfect vengeance when every measure of human justice failed. I now believe that the reason Sandra never required fitting retribution to appease her wrath and soften her bitterness was because she never felt those things in the first place.

I once heard Sheila Walsh, one of the primary speakers at Women of Faith conferences, testify that, "to live as a Christian woman means living a life of joy mixed with sorrow." Sandra's experience that year was no exception. Shortly before Christmas (on her birthday, no less!) Brian asked her to be his wife. As we gathered for the holidays, we all rejoiced with the couple over their recent engagement, and only occasionally would Sandra's happiness give way to moments of grief. It was her first Christmas alongside Brian as her intended; it was the first Christmas without her son. It was a poignant, bittersweet time of celebration intertwined with mourning, but of all the emotions Sandra displayed, never once did I see her give in to anger or resentment.

As the months went by, the passing of time helped

lessen the grief, and by the time we reached the wedding day the following spring, we were all able to celebrate with undiluted joy. I expect in Sandra's heart Andrew was absent in physical presence only, confident that from his own unique vantage point he was nonetheless an equally jubilant witness.

God is so faithful to restore loss and, as He promises, will repay you for "the years the locusts have eaten" (Joel 2:25 NIV). What a privilege it was to witness Him fulfill those promises so quickly in the life of this couple. A season of loneliness had been replaced by a life of perfect partnership. The delight of celebrating the arrival of not one but two baby boys. Given that the couple had to contend with health issues, Brian's grueling travel schedule, and what obstetricians refer to as "advanced maternal age," the long-awaited arrival of these precious boys was especially welcomed.

The years Sandra sacrificed as a working mother to provide for her son were exchanged for a new career as a full-time wife and mother. With characteristic dedication she embraced the task of raising her boys and making a home for her family. As she had always done, she continued to work hard for her loved ones, but now her outward efforts were directed toward her preschool mothers' group, the boys' school, and increased commitments at church. Not content to simply nurture her own children, her home was opened as a welcome haven for virtually all the neighborhood children. Shortly after their older son was born, I looked from Brian, the loving husband and devoted father, to their beautiful new baby, to Sandra, and remarked, "Your life has been rather Job-like, hasn't it?"

While Sandra can still remember at one time she never expected to laugh or feel joy again, I've watched as she goes through life with the happy heart that comes from a thankful heart. I know she counts herself as one truly blessed. At the same time I've witnessed others sacrifice their own joy to bitterness as they carry much greater grudges over relatively small offenses. One day I finally confessed to Sandra how much I admired her as a my role model of truly heroic forgiveness. Of all the unexpected moments I've witnessed in her life, not one came as big a surprise as the reply she then gave me: "I'm so lucky," she said.

Lucky? I thought. *After all she had endured, she feels lucky?*

She explained, "God just kept me from having a hatred for this man. All the things people told me I should expect to feel, I never did. I feel that he just made an unfortunate mistake with devastating consequences."

I was humbled and convicted as I recalled all the times I had been just as foolish, just as thoughtless, and even just as reckless, and but for the grace of God the mistakes I made could have had just as horrendous outcomes. Until that moment I had always presumed somehow that I had the right to extend forgiveness to others, when the truth is, in God's eyes I am no less guilty, and certainly no more deserving of His forgiveness. Sandra understood that though, and because she did she rested in the assurance of her own reconciliation to God, as well as her son's reconciliation to God. Finally, unbelievably, she even experienced reconciliation with her son's murderer.

I have since come to the conclusion that Sandra wholly enjoys all the blessings God has given her because she first accepted His miraculous gift of forgiveness. Looking back over all I have learned from this extraordinary woman, once again I realize what an even more extraordinary God we worship. What a limited understanding of forgiveness I have always had! I truly never expected forgiveness to look like this. Until now, I always assumed it was something we decided on our own—that in an act of will over feelings, it was up to us to *choose* forgiveness. I never fully grasped that forgiveness was a gift God could *give* us. How unexpected that in a measure of extravagant grace God could take away completely the burdens Sandra expected she would carry, and instead place in her hands more than she could ever wish to hold. To me that is the most miraculous part of all—He does the very same for each one of us.

The Case of the Unfaithful Wife

JIM BROOKS

Two years ago I could never have written this story. The fact that I am now putting it on paper proves to me what miracles can take place through a transformation of the human spirit.

When Nancy and I were married, I gave her a beautiful little bedside clock with a sprightly musical alarm to wake us up mornings. On the back I had engraved her initials and under them, "Won—1951. One—1952."

The clock seemed to become a symbol of our love and life together. In time we had two wonderful children and a home in the suburbs of a Midwestern city. Nancy was a good mother and homemaker. She also found an outlet for her enormous energy in various community causes.

We differed in our religious beliefs, however. I'd been brought up in a church-centered family; she was indifferent to most matters of faith and believed only that some impersonal Force created the universe. She was such a realist that sometimes her honest bluntness made me wince.

"In a real crisis, Jim," she once told me, "I wonder if your faith would be of any help to you."

Nancy was unhappy that I had to travel so much for my firm. At first I brought home little gifts for her from these trips, but I stopped doing that when my travels became such a regular part of our lives.

And then came the first time that I sensed something wrong in our marriage. When we went to bed one night, I noticed the clock was not on our night stand. For some reason this sent a little chill through me. When I questioned her, Nancy mumbled something about its needing repairs. For the first time it occurred to me that she'd been depressed and listless recently. Although my work took me out of town three of the next four weeks, I resolved that when I was home I would be more attentive and sensitive. And now that I was conscious of it, her behavior did seem erratic. There were extremes of irritability and heights of exhilaration, which seemed unnatural.

One night while looking for our checkbook, I opened Nancy's bureau drawer. Pushed far into a back corner was the small clock. I took it to Nancy.

"I thought you said it was being repaired."

"Oh, did I?" Her eyes were bright, brittle.

"What's wrong, Nancy? Something's badly wrong."

Nancy's brittle look was gone; her lips were trembling. "You're right, Jim. Something's wrong," she said, dabbing angrily at her tear-filled eyes. "I . . . haven't been true to you. It's . . . well . . . what more can I say?"

I looked at her, bewildered, unbelieving. Numbly, I tried to get her to put the facts together.

"You don't know him, Jim. He's an old friend from college days who looked me up one time while you were gone. It was a mistake. It's all over." Nancy suddenly looked a hundred years old. I wanted to hit her. Instead, I strode out of the house.

I walked for hours. *Why? Why? Why?* The question drummed in my mind. Why had Nancy done this to me? Divorce was obviously my only choice. But the children! The pain inside me was sickening. *How could she do this to them?*

It was late when I returned home. I slept on the sofa and was up and out before daybreak, leaving a note that business would keep me away a week or more. That part was true enough—there were always customers to call on—but in the back of my mind was already the idea of going to see Harry.

Harry Brand, an air force buddy from World War II, was now pastor of a church five or six hours' drive from us. He had been an usher at our wedding, and I knew he was a person I could talk to.

When I arrived, he greeted me warmly. "Let's go over to the house where we can talk, Jim."

"I'm not here on a social call, Harry."

He gave me a long look. "I see. Well, let's sit down here then."

I drew a deep breath and plunged ahead. "You know Nancy and me fairly well. We've had a good marriage. Well, it's over. Nancy's had an affair."

Harry fixed me with the mild gaze. "And she wants to leave you for this other man?"

"No. She didn't say that. I don't know what she wants. I mean . . . when someone breaks the most sacred vow there is, that's it. Isn't it? I mean, what's left?"

Moments passed before Harry spoke. "Jim, let me begin by saying that I sense your pain. The fact that you have such pain is an encouraging sign. Too many married people today are indifferent about adultery. But tell me, Jim, could part of that wound be to your pride?"

I frowned, started to make a quick retort, then checked it. "I don't know. Nancy and I had something fine together, and now it's gone forever. That's what hurts the most," I said.

"If you are completely convinced that what you and Nancy had is gone forever, then you do not believe in the Christian faith."

"How can you say that?"

Because a Christian believes in and practices forgiveness. I know Nancy well enough to believe that if she committed the sin of adultery, she, too, is dying inside and is aching for your forgiveness.

"All the forgiveness in the world can't alter the facts."

"Then you do not really believe that Christ meant what he said."

"But why would she do this to me?"

"Perhaps she felt you'd stopped loving her. You told me yourself last year you were traveling nearly half the time. A man can get so busy making a living that he starts taking the important things for granted. Nancy's one of the important things."

"Then you suggest I go home and tell her I forgive her, just like that?"

"Not 'just like that.' I suggest you first ask God to grant you this spirit of forgiveness—He's the only one who can do it."

Harry got out of his chair, walked around the desk and placed his big hands on my shoulders. "Believe me, Jim, I've encountered this situation often enough to know that if you can't forgive—or won't—then you have only two other choices, both bad. You can live together for the children in an atmosphere of bitterness and self-pity—or break up your home altogether.

"Face up to something, will you, Jim? We're all sinners

in one way or another. The Lord may look upon your sin of pride as severely as He does Nancy's breaking one of His commandments."

I felt angry. Harry made it sound as though I were as much at fault as Nancy.

Rebellious thoughts churned inside me all week. Why should I accept any blame for this mess? I had been faithful to Nancy. I was the one who had steered the family into spiritual activities.

It was early Friday afternoon when I pulled into our driveway. The dishwasher was clanging away when I opened the front door, and Nancy must not have heard me. In fact, I had stepped into the living room before I saw her. She was on her knees in front of the sofa.

All at once I knew that God had granted me that priceless gift of forgiveness. I felt something fresh wash through me. The anger and bitterness were simply gone. I took a step toward her.

And at last she heard me. She jumped to her feet, long brown hair falling over her shoulders. Her eyes were red-rimmed and swollen.

I took her in my arms, and her sobs broke my heart.

Harry was right, of course. Love had returned—if possible, deeper than before. If our friends notice that I'm home oftener on weekends, that we never miss church anymore, they don't attach any significance to it. But Nancy and I do. Today Nancy knows that God is not just a Force presiding over an impersonal universe; she knows He is a Father intimately concerned with every detail of our lives and relationships. And I know a little bit more about the promise I took on when I so proudly ordered the word "One" engraved on the little musical clock.

The clock? It's out of its hiding place and back where it belongs beside our bed.

The St. Patrick's Day Fiasco

ELEANOR M. BEHMAN

I had always considered myself a caring, watchful mom. I'd even been accused of being overprotective at times. But I just needed to know that my children were safe under my care. After all, I reasoned, the Lord had entrusted them to me, and he would surely want me to do my very best. I took this job seriously and made sure I knew the children's whereabouts at all times. But it turns out that moms can't always keep their children out of trouble—we just have to do our best and hope that, when mistakes are made, angels take over where we leave off.

My husband worked nights for many years, and I was a stay-at-home mom. When our daughter and son were eight and five years old, our wonderful third child made her entrance into the world. I had really wanted another baby, and after trying to convince my husband for a year, he finally caved in. Kristine May Behman was born May 31, 1967. She was, as I saw it, my bonus baby.

As the nurse held our infant daughter in the hospital nursery and fed her Karo water, she would croon and say she was feeding her chicken soup. After watching this for a few days, the name "chicken soup" sort of stuck, and from then on our Krissy had a nickname. Since then we've shortened it to "Soup," and everyone knows who we're talking about.

Soup was an adorable little imp, and as a three-year-old could be sweet and entertaining, or she could test us to our limits. Sometimes she did both at once.

It was a clear spring day in 1970, and my husband was away at work. The day before, he and the older children had cleaned out the basement playroom, so I didn't think twice about letting sweet little Soup play down there alone. In fact, I was pleased because she usually wanted to be around lots of people and hardly ever played by herself. I thought this would do her some good.

This particular day I was busy baking in the kitchen, so I let Soup play until naptime. After a little while, I went downstairs to get her and brought her up to her room. Little did I know she was as clever as a secret agent hiding evidence. I laid her in bed and went back downstairs to finish my baking.

I could hear Soup talking and playing, and after awhile I went upstairs to check on her. I was shocked to find her sitting up, smiling from ear to ear, smearing green pain all over her face! She was apparently playing with "makeup" like mommy, using bright green paint for "cosmetics." I anxiously looked in her hand and saw that she was clutching a small pot of paint-by-numbers paint, which had gone unnoticed when the playroom had been cleaned.

Not knowing whether to laugh or cry, I spontaneously did a little of both. My next few frightening moments were filled with anxious prayers. I didn't know if she had swallowed any paint, so I prayed that if she had, the paint was not toxic. As I frantically scrubbed her face, Soup popped out her little tongue, which was also coated green. I felt guilty that I hadn't noticed the paint lying around in easy reach of my little girl's hands. It was a lesson in childproofing I knew I'd never forget!

I wanted to get Soup to a hospital as soon as possible since she might have swallowed a substantial amount of paint. I rushed downstairs, and, since I didn't have my own car, I called my sister to see if she could pick us up. But her car wouldn't start. So I called my husband at work only to discover that he was out of the building at a meeting. Not knowing how the paint was affecting my little girl, I couldn't wait at home any longer, so I called the police. While I waited for an officer to arrive, I wrapped the small pot of paint in a napkin and bundled my green-faced child in a blanket.

The police arrived quickly and, in spite of the obvious guilt I felt at this horrible lapse in good motherhood, the patrolman laughed kindly as he looked at the paint-smeared three-year-old in my arms. He tried to reassure me by saying that his daughter had gotten ahold of his wife's lipstick and written all over the bathroom wall. I appreciated his effort, but felt that my plight was much more serious.

We rushed to the hospital with the sirens blaring and my nerves jangling. I was ushered into a room where a doctor evaluated the situation. I handed him the paint so they could analyze it, and they took Soup into an adjoining room. In those days, parents weren't allowed to be in the room while their children were tended to. I paced the floor in the waiting room and prayed that Soup would be all right. My heart lurched as I heard her screaming for me while they pumped the paint from her stomach. Based on her green tongue, the doctors felt that she may have swallowed enough to make her ill. They could not take any chances. The lab, in the meantime, analyzed the paint and found it to be nontoxic.

I was grateful, but exhausted. Everything that had led up to this moment in a cold, antiseptic hospital room proved to be too much for me. My nerves were frazzled, and I cried freely as I came down from my "mothers can do no wrong" pedestal. I had to admit that we are actually human, and even when we think we've covered all the angles with our children, accidents happen. We can only try to do our best, learn from life's experiences, and try not to repeat the same mistakes. I went home and moved everything from my cleaning cabinet up to the highest shelf, out of the reach of little hands.

It wasn't until later that evening, when I settled down a bit, that I realized it was St. Patrick's Day. Soup had given a whole new meaning to "the wearing o' the green"! What a ridiculous picture we must have made on that fast and furious ride to the hospital: A hysterical mother with flour on her face and a little, green-faced child, speeding down the street in a police car.

I saw no humor in it at the time, but now, every St. Patrick's Day, Soup and I laugh about how we once celebrated in a very unusual way. Throughout the years, I've tried to remind myself that even when we make mistakes—and we all do—we can learn from them and maybe even laugh about them later on.

CHAPTER **3**

Repairing Relationships

You are a forgiving God. You are kind and full of mercy.
You do not become angry quickly, and you have great love
(Nehemiah 9:17 NCV).

Relationships sometimes are broken. By jealousy. By abuse. By harsh words. By neglect. Even by mistake. These all-too-precious relationships are too rare and too important to leave broken, though. They deserve our constant attention and our every effort to maintain them or repair them when needed. Forgiveness is the great healing balm for relationship schisms. It's the super glue that holds us together. Apply it liberally.

Football and Forgiveness

RACHAEL PHILLIPS

L et's buy season football tickets and go to the games." Steve, my boyfriend, could hardly contain his excitement. "They're only eighteen dollars!"

Somehow I managed to change the subject as we walked hand in hand to our dormitories. Flame-tipped maples and golden tulip poplars waved their royal banners at us, but I barely noticed the beauty of the Indiana University campus that fall day in 1971. Instead, my stomach twisted as I thought about my pitiful bank balance.

Later I made myself face facts. The summer before I had hoarded every nickel and dime I earned as a waitress on the graveyard shift at Denny's. Still, the extra costs for my music education courses had drained my financial reserves far more than I expected. I refused to ask Steve to pay for the tickets, even though I knew my boyfriend would not miss the money at all. Yet how could I tell him I possessed a grand total of sixty-six dollars to cover toothpaste, school supplies, and laundry for four months?

Besides, I hated football. To me, it resembled a synchronized gang rumble. Any game in which people smashed and trampled each other into the mud for a pointy ball was not worth a penny, let alone eighteen precious dollars.

On the other hand, I would hand-wash my jeans and brush my teeth with soap, if that would allow me to purchase an eighteen-dollar ticket for the university's concert series. I dreamed of the world-famous orchestras and soloists who would play the classical music I loved. I pictured Steve, tall and handsome in his navy blue double-breasted coat—the one he wore on our first date—calling for me at my dorm. I, wearing my one long dress, would float into the elegant, red-curtained auditorium on his arm. Together we would listen to violins, cellos, and a Steinway piano playing swirling waves of music that would surround us with romance.

How could he expect me to spend my hard-earned money freezing to death in a stadium with thousands of howling fans who didn't know Mendelssohn from the Monkees?

I hoped Steve would just *forget* about the tickets.

Right. No enthusiastic eighteen-year-old boy forgets about football tickets.

"But I don't know anything about the game!" I tried to look as sweet and pathetic as I could.

"I'll teach you!" he offered. "I know you'll love it as much as I do!"

I knew I wouldn't.

But I loved so many things about Steve—the smiles that crinkled the corners of his mouth, the strong, gentle way he talked to me, his listening ear. He was the first guy I had dated who shared my Christian faith and interest in academics. I hoped our budding relationship would go on . . . and on. But something told me that if we were to share a future, football would play a part in it. So I forgave him for his misguided obsession, and I tried not to roll my eyes when he regaled me with endless tales of tackles and touchdowns. Together we stopped by the college athletic office. I surrendered my check, saying a silent, hopeless prayer for my finances.

As we walked home past the huge auditorium, I could not resist a longing look at the posted schedule of concert events. Mozart. Beethoven. Haydn. I tried not to think of the incredible music I would miss.

"Oh, by the way . . ." Steve pulled something from his pocket. His blue eyes twinkled. "I bought two season tickets to the concert series. Would you like to go with me?"

Thirty-two years later, is it any wonder I *still* love him—and football?

Let Bygones Be Bygones

RENIE (SZILAK) BURGHARDT

I was born in the Bacska region of Hungary, a region that became a part of Yugoslavia after World War II. Known as Vojvodina today, it is now apart of Northern Serbia. Many ethnic Hungarians still live there, including many of my relatives.

When the guns of Tito's communist Partisans echoed through the hills above the village, my grandparents, who were raising me, decided to leave for safer surroundings. So they packed up our horse-drawn wagon with as much as they could, and we left the region. However, safer surroundings eluded us, and the day after Christmas 1944, the city where we were living at the time was bombed.

My grandfather was the rock of our family. He had been a small town judge for many years, and his strong sense of justice, unwavering faith in God, and strong love for his family was always evident.

That night of the day after Christmas 1944, when I was eight years old, warplanes could be heard approaching the city we were in. Sirens shrieked their warnings in the darkness and the deafening roar of exploding bombs filled the air. Our house began to tremble, and Grandfather grabbed me and ordered Grandma to follow him into the closet, where I sank down in a corner covering my ears with my hands, trying to shut out the terrifying noise. My grandmother pulled me into her arms, while Grandpa pulled the closet door shut. The house shook and pieces of plaster and dust fell from the ceiling onto our heads as the house began to crumble.

"Grandpa, I can't breathe," I cried out, panic gripping me by the throat. "Are we going to die?"

"Pray, sweetheart, pray. God will protect us," Grandfather said, shielding us with his body, and leading us in prayer throughout the entire ordeal, the prayer calming me. And when the bombing finally stopped, we could hear people above the rubble. People who came to dig us out, to see if we were alive. Miraculously, the closet had stayed mostly intact, and because we were in it, our lives were saved. We found out later many had not been as fortunate, and together with Grandpa we said a grateful prayer of thanks, and continued living in the war-torn environment as best as we could. But we were together, and we had Grandpa as our guardian and protector.

The end of the war in 1945 held no jubilation for us because the Red Soviet army was now holding our country hostage in the arms of communism. My grandfather became an active member of the Small Holders Party, and often spoke out against new atrocities being committed against his countrymen, the common people.

New elections forthcoming, he actively campaigned against the communist party. A neighbor, who we knew was a big communist supporter, reported him.

A few days later, two men of the secret police came to our house to take him in for questioning. My grandfather, aware that people taken in for questioning were never seen again, asked the men if he could wash his hands before going with them, since he had been working in the garden. The men agreed. When he didn't emerge from the bathroom shortly, the men pushed the door open. The water in the sink was still running, but Grandfather was gone. He had jumped out the window and fled on foot.

After my grandfather went into hiding, life became extremely hard for Grandmother and me. We lived on soup made from vegetables grown in our garden and never knew when the secret police would show up in hopes of finding my grandfather. Sometimes they came in the middle of the night, breaking down the door. Fear became our constant companion, but constant prayer kept us going.

For two years, Grandfather managed to elude capture by hiding out on some nearby farms, and although at times he sent word that he was safe, most of the time we didn't know his whereabouts. Grandma and I missed him terribly. The thought that we might never be together again upset me, and I constantly prayed that we would be reunited.

In 1947, new elections were being held in our country and the radio blared the news that the communist party had been defeated. Celebrations erupted in the streets of our village, with none of us realizing that the communist party, backed by the Soviet troops, did not intend to give up power, elections or no elections. My hope that Grandfather could come home and we could be a family again was not realized.

In November of 1947, a man was sent by Grandfather to get us in the middle of the night. By the time the sun rose, we had arrived at a place near the Austrian border where a large group of ethnic Germans were about to be deported from Hungary. (The term "ethnic cleansing" hadn't been coined yet.)

Grandfather was already there to meet us, through some secret arrangement. My heart leaped with joy when I saw Grandfather. He looked into my eyes lovingly and hugged me tightly, but we knew we were still in danger. We were about to be smuggled out of our homeland as ethnic Germans. Of course, we didn't dare to breathe a sigh of relief until we crossed into Austria.

When we finally crossed the border, we were trucked off to a refugee camp, a self-contained world of old army barracks lined up as far as the eyes could see. Shortly after we arrived, they filled our tin can eating utensils with hot cabbage and potato soup to appease our hunger. Then we were given warmer clothes donated by kind Americans. Inside the barracks were cardboard cubicles furnished with sleeping cots and horsehair blankets. One of those cubicles became our home for the next four years. But the important thing was we were finally together again! But Grandfather remained fearful even in the refugee camp that the long arm of Communism could still reach out and snatch him back.

In 1951, we finally received the notice we had been waiting for. We had passed all the health screening and were approved to immigrate to the United States of America, where Grandfather was able to relax and live his life in grateful peace. I was fourteen.

We settled in a large city in Ohio, where my grandparents went to work and I went to school. There were many Hungarians in the area and we soon joined a Hungarian church there. Two years later, who should we run into at that church but the man who had tried to get Grandfather arrested back in Hungary. We knew he had succeeded with many others and had been the cause of their imprisonment. We also learned that he and his family later had also found disfavor with the new communist government, and the man's brother had been imprisoned. So he and his large family of a wife and five children had fled into Austria, too, eventually ending up in America. Maybe it was fate.

Our minister at the church called a meeting between Grandfather and this man, at the man's request. It seemed he had something to say.

"I am very sorry for what I did to you, Jozsef," the man told Grandfather. "I have asked God to forgive me for all my acts against my countrymen. And I ask you to forgive me too. But I will understand if you cannot."

Grandfather, of course, did forgive him, and they prayed together as Father Imre blessed them both.

"He is just afraid that you will turn him in for being the traitor he is," Grandmother said, after Grandfather told us what had transpired. "Perhaps. Perhaps not," Grandfather answered thoughtfully. "But I can't be the judge of this man. I leave that up to God. We are safe now, and he has a large family to look after. It's for the best to let bygones be bygones and go on with our lives in peace. Holding a grudge harbors hate and unhappiness. And I don't want hate in my heart. I am happy we are in America, where we can live in freedom. I thank God for making that possible for us. And even for Paul and his family."

I have never forgotten Grandfather's words. They have been an inspiration throughout my life. Forgiveness is better than revenge, for it brings peace to the heart of the one who forgives.

Last Request

ZARETTE BEARD

As a newlywed, I was one of the few people who was looking forward to spending time with my in-laws (or outlaws, for that matter). I just assumed we all would get along beautifully as one big happy family. I couldn't have been more wrong. All family members, myself included, brought their own ideas to the relationships. I had high hopes for my father-in-law and I to be close friends, but it was just not to be.

Every time we were in the same room, a power struggle reared its ugly head and we argued. Every single time, no matter how hard I tried to look the other way. I was certain he was deliberately picking fights with me, but who would actually do that, and who would believe me anyway? Not wanting to put my husband in the middle, I was in a no-win situation. I was angry and saddened over the loss of a potential friendship with this man. I grew to resent him and tried to avoid getting together as much as possible. As my husband knew, his father was no picnic to get along with, but I was still confused over my perceived persecution. I had expected better.

Then we got a call telling us the man was dying of cancer. When you get that call, all bets are off. We jumped into the car and drove out of state to see him. I had already convinced myself he would be scared and angry about dying, so I should just take whatever he was going to throw at me and be quiet. After all, the man was dying. Firmly committed to absorbing whatever he would say, I smiled when I saw him. We had only been at the house a short time when he called everyone into the dining room.

I will never forget what happened next. Right there in front of everyone, he admitted to starting fights with me on purpose! He detailed all of the times he started an argument with me and explained that it was his own insecurities, not my fault. In that moment, I felt so completely vindicated and justified, I was certain I would jump from my seat and point an accusing finger at him with a loud "Ah-Ha! Told you all! I was *right!* But, thankfully, that's not what happened at all. I looked at this man, really looked and saw the sadness in his face mixed with the vulnerability that enveloped him. Before I could stop myself, I got up from my chair, put my arms around him, thanked him, and told him it was all okay. We cried together, he and I, and in that moment it all changed. The distance between us, the tension and hostility were gone. It was as if we regarded each other for the first time. We had a good talk after that and exchanged a few laughs and knowing glances. I grew closer to my father-in-law in two days than I had in a decade.

If you ever get the chance, choose forgiveness over vindication. Forgiveness transcends space and time. It reaches back into the past to heal and reaches forward to build a bridge. Forgiveness. What an amazing gift!

Forgiveness with a Hitch

PATTI MAGUIRE ARMSTRONG

It was one of those frustrating times when you are try-ing to leave on a trip but cannot seem to get on the road. In this case, I was moving my third son Tyler to col-lege, two-and-a-half hours away from Bismarck to Fargo, North Dakota. We were all sad to see him go. He was transferring to North Dakota State University after a year at the local community college. One of my other sons, Luke, was sharing an apartment with him, so I was com-forted to know the two of them would be roommates.

Also leaving with us was Tyler's girlfriend, Jessie. Although we had a large family of ten kids, Jessie had managed to find a place in everyone's heart. Jessie was also transferring to Fargo and planned to drive her car behind Tyler. Both had decided to move up early during the summer in order to get jobs and be settled when the school year started. But that morning there was one delay after another. Just when we thought everything was final-ly ready, Jessie said she had to run to the bank to get some money. While we waited, she phoned to tell us that her bankcard was lost. Tyler suggested just leaving ahead of her since we would be driving slowly and she could catch up with us later in the day.

Jessie tried to remain calm but the tears came. Not until then did I realize she had actually never driven out of town on her own. She was not even sure of the directions. Then there was the stress of running late and losing her bankcard. But perhaps the real reason for her tears was what she was leaving behind. Her mother— her best friend—had died only nine months earlier. Jessie was a strong and sensible girl, but there were times she missed her mother terribly. Embarking on such a milestone as this was surely one of those times. Her parents had divorced a couple years before her mother died. There were resentments, both real and imagined, and emotions sometimes ran high between Jessie and her father. When she asked him to wake her up before he left for work that morning, she had expected him to come and say good-bye. Instead, he called her name before the door banged closed, and he drove off to the fire station where he worked. Her father did not want her to go away to college, but Jessie had expected he would still want to say good-bye to her. With no mother to help her prepare, and feeling emotionally abandoned by her father, Jessie was carrying a heavy weight that morning.

Realizing she didn't want to drive up alone, we agreed to wait for her. Jessie never did find her bankcard, but she decided she would report it missing after we got to Fargo. (Someone found it and turned it in later that day.) Then, finally we were on the road, almost two hours behind our original plan. Just a mile from our home, Tyler pulled into a convenience store to buy drinks and snacks. I complained, impatient to get going. "I'll just be a minute," he promised.

A few minutes later, it seemed we were really ready this time. But then, as our van descended a steep drive-way onto the street, the trailer hitch scraped the concrete and came off. "Oh no," I said, wondering if we were even roadworthy with this sort of occurrence. Tyler hauled out a hammer and screwdriver.

"Don't worry," he assured me and plopped down under the hitch. "I know what's wrong and I can fix it." I returned to the van and waited through this latest delay. After a few minutes I looked out the back window and saw Jessie's dad, wearing his fireman's uniform, giving Jessie a big hug. Our hitch had come off kitty-corner from the fire station where he worked. He had looked out the window and spotted Jessie's car parked behind our van and hurried out the door to say good-bye to his daughter. Whatever fear or resentments he had over Jessie leaving melted away when he looked out the window and saw her standing outside her car waiting to leave.

A hug good-bye from her father meant the world to

Jessie. In spite of all the factors that complicated their relationship now, Jessie loved him. When she talked of her childhood memories, they were filled with love and admiration for her father—the props he helped build for her dance recitals or the time she slipped away from him skiing and he frantically looked for her. A cloud overshadowed this next chapter on her life because she was leaving town without saying good-bye to her dad.

It had to be divine intervention that brought Jessie and her father together at the very last minute. For some reason, Tyler didn't pick up snacks at the store we had already passed. And for some reason, our hitch came off within view of the fire station. We needed to be there, stuck for a few minutes in order for the good-bye to take place.

It's always good to forgive others without a hitch, but in this case, it was the hitch that brought reconciliation between a father and daughter. And just a couple days later, Jessie's dad decided to drive out to Fargo. After spending the day helping her get settled, his reluctance to see her leave home was replaced with a new feeling. "I'm actually kind of excited for you," he admitted. So, a second good-bye took place just a few days later, but this time, without a hitch.

A Short Step Over the Edge

MURIEL WILSON JACKSON

The other day a woman told me she was leaving her husband, an alcoholic. "It would take a miracle to help him," she said.

"Then let's pray for one," I suggested. And I told her my story.

Years ago when I married Joe he was bright, handsome, and ambitious. But somewhere in the early years of our marriage he lost control of his drinking. We began moving from place to place; from job to job. The bleary-eyed man who shared my home bore small resemblance to the charming young man I had married.

Finally in 1953 we came back to live in the small Texas town where I was born. An old aunt gave us living quarters in a shack by the river. Meanwhile, Joe worked just enough to buy liquor and we barely existed.

Joe was not a mean drunk, just a hopeless one. In his half sober moments he often begged me to leave him for my own good, and then panicked when he thought I might.

I had been raised to believe in prayer. God answers earnest prayer, I thought, and I certainly prayed earnestly for Joe! I was so confident in God, in the beginning, so positive He would help us.

But as the years passed and Joe slipped steadily down, I felt this bedrock of my own life slipping from me too. Where was God? Why didn't He hear?

And if there were no God then I saw no reason to live. I had no children, no friends any more, no hope for Joe. I kept thinking of the swift Llano River swirling past our door. How quickly it would be done!

Then came the dreadful night when I knew I could do it. Joe had dragged himself from bed to go out and get the bottle he could not live without. I begged him not to go, but he just looked at me.

After he left, a fierce anger took possession of me, and I cried until I was exhausted. And then a deep depression set in—a terrible, hollow, helpless feeling. I ran outside and headed for the stream.

The moon slid behind a cloud just as I reached the swift deep pools below the Slab in the Llano. The water made an ominous sound as it surged into the whirlpool.

At the very edge of the water something restrained me. Long religious habit forced me to my knees on the rough wet sand to ask forgiveness from the God I no longer believed in.

How long I remained in this attitude of prayer, hands clasped, head bowed, I do not know. Still my determination never wavered.

I raised my head, ready to stand and take the short step over the edge. Then I blinked my eyes to be sure I was seeing clearly. The water, which had been inky black when I knelt, was a flaming, scarlet red.

Too terrified to breathe I stared at this swirling blood-colored pool. Over the rocks, past the Slab, poured a red cascade. I watched, transfixed, then I saw what had happened.

Across the river was the old farm house—my birthplace—long abandoned. Bright red light was streaming from every window. Fire! But what could have started it? The house—a shack worse than ours—was uninhabitable.

As I watched, my heart pounding in my throat, the eerie red light began to dim. For the first time I felt the sand, hard and wet beneath my knees. But still I could not stand. My brain reeled with thoughts too large for it. The house where life began for me—began through no effort of my own—was this a sign that my life was not my own to take? The blood-red water, did it have the same message? I had been bought with a price. I was not my own. I belonged to Another. None of this came to me in so many words. All my conscious mind was aware of was the mighty hand of God, closer than I had ever felt it.

I put my head on the ground and sobbed my heart out. But these were not the angry frustrated tears I had shed earlier in the evening, crying for things I had lost. These were thankful tears, tears of shame, tears of joy.

Then I finally rose and started home. The same river sang a new song, a happy song as it hurried to join the Colorado in its rush to the open sea. Somehow I knew that everything would be all right. I knew there was no problem I need face alone.

When I arrived home I found Joe lying across the bed fully clothed, in an alcoholic stupor. I removed his shoes and straightened him out on the bed. That night, instead of going to the cot in the corner where I always slept when he was drunk, I lay down beside him. I held my poor helpless husband in my arms until the shaking stopped and his snores told me that he was sleeping. Exhausted, I fell asleep too.

Joe had been seeing a doctor at a small clinic in a nearby town. As I served him black coffee next morning his eyes followed me. "Will you come with me to the doctor's today?" he asked suddenly.

The doctor was a kind-faced man who stood up and shook hands with me. He had been treating Joe for arthritis, migraine headaches, and other ills that his mis-treated body suffered. But that morning, to our surprise, he didn't ask about Joe's physical condition at all. He spent the entire session talking to us about Alcoholics Anonymous. He told how A.A. had helped many problem drinkers find sobriety.

Suddenly, as if on impulse, the doctor stood up and asked us to follow him. Across the hall he led us into a room marked, "No Visitors."

On a narrow bed lay a figure covered, except for the head, with a white hospital sheet. The face was almost invisible under a layer of thick white ointment, but even so we could see that it was horribly burned. The eyebrows and lashes were gone and most of the hair was burned away. We stared in silence, wondering why the doctor was showing us this.

Outside again, he told us who the man was—another notorious town drunk of this little community. He said the man had crawled into the old Wilson house, out by the Slab, the night before. In some manner, probably with a cigarette, he had set fire to the pile of ragged quilts he lay on. He was dragged out by some fishermen, but it was too late. It was a miracle that he had lived this long.

"These are the things," said the doctor, looking at Joe, "that happen to men with your particular problem. For an alcoholic it must be complete abstinence, a mental institution, or an early grave. In A.A., other alcoholics will show you how to overcome your problem."

As we drove home, we both were silent. I didn't know

what Joe was thinking, but I felt sure the doctor's words had made a strong impression. There was a flicker of hope in his pale blue eyes.

Six weeks later Joe found his way into the Alcoholics Anonymous group in San Antonio. A.A. became our way of life. Joe turned his will and his life over to the care of God, and God did an awful lot with the seven years that were left of it. He became a valuable citizen in our community, a member of the Bishops Committee at St. Luke's Episcopal Church, the president of the local Rotary Club.

He was appointed Rehabilitation Counselor at our state's tough maximum security hospital. He worked and lived among criminal alcoholics, filled with love and humility and the grace of God. No one knows how many broken homes and broken hearts he helped to mend, but the record of recoveries among his alcoholic patients was outstanding.

Joe became the happiest, most contented man I've ever known, even when he entered the hospital in Dallas in 1959 with Hodgkins Disease. He knew he was dying, yet his thin body could hardly contain the love and joy that filled his soul.

"God has been awfully good to us," he said to me. "What if this had happened seven years ago?"

This is the story I told the woman who wanted to leave her husband. I also told her it was wrong to say there are no modern miracles; miracles still happen. I know, for one of forgiveness happened for me.

Change of Heart

STEVEN POULTER

The emergency-room doctor gave it to me straight. "Your kidneys are failing," she said. I stared at my wife, Coreena. Instinctively, I sought her hand. I'm a big guy, a long-haul truck driver, a guy's guy. But I was having trouble keeping it together. How could this be? I was twenty-seven years old. Still, I'd had several health problems and this was the result.

I got on the phone immediately to my family and close friends. Partly to let them know, but partly, too, to find out if anyone close to me was a potential transplant match. I was on the bottom rung of the kidney donor list. The specialist I consulted said, "You have five years to get a transplant, or . . ." He didn't need to say more.

I called everyone. Well, almost everyone. There was my mom. But I couldn't call her. We hadn't spoken in years.

My parents divorced when I was eight years old. That hurt bad enough. But then Mom told me I had to live with Dad. That really hurt. "I won't go!" I screamed at her.

But two weeks later she packed my things. "You don't

have a choice," she said, tight-lipped. "You're going."

How can she do this to me? I thought. Maybe it was part of the custody agreement, maybe it was some arrangement set up by the judge. No one would ever explain it to me.

I got into the car with Dad that day and we headed from Oklahoma to his new home in Kansas. The drive across the flat, featureless landscape seemed endless. I just stared out the window, growing angrier and angrier. By the time we reached Dad's home, I was a seething ball of hurt and rage. I wanted nothing to do with Mom. If she loved me, how could she send me away?

I rarely saw her after that and only spoke with her sporadically. Our conversations weren't pleasant. From my end, there were mostly clipped words and silence. I deliberately shut her out of my life.

I swore to myself that when I grew up and married, there'd be no one more devoted to family than me. Coreena and our three girls became my world. Even when I was on the road hauling loads halfway across the country, there was never a night when I didn't call to say how much I loved them. I spent every minute with them that I could. I didn't have time for Mom, especially after I got sick.

But Coreena finally told Mom about my condition. One day she phoned. Coreena answered.

"Tell her I'm not here," I said.

By then things had gotten tough for us. What could she do? Pity us? I was too sick to work. I needed twelve hours of dialysis treatments per week. Coreena and I had already gone through our savings, and my first disability check was five months away. Coreena had taken a job at a fast-food restaurant, but it didn't pay nearly enough. I'd always believed that a man's job was to provide for his family. And now all I could do was lie around, too weak to even play with our three girls. The last thing I wanted was to talk to Mom.

"Your mom offered to let us move in with her," Coreena said, after she hung up. "She offered to help with the girls."

"No way!" I said.

But she called again and again. Finally I had no choice but to accept her offer. Temporarily, I reminded myself, until my disability came through. The girls needed looking after and we were flat broke.

So, with a chip on my shoulder, Coreena and I and our three girls moved into Mom's mobile home, five hours away in Texas.

Temporarily. There were nine of us in a three-bedroom home. Mom had remarried and had two teenage children. It was all I could do to watch her with her new family—with children she hadn't tossed aside—and keep from erupting. I hid out in a bedroom when I wasn't taking dialysis treatments.

Coreena would try to coax me out of the room. "Come on, Steven, join us," she'd say. "Your mom made a wonderful meatloaf for dinner."

"Tell her I'm too tired to eat at the table," I told Coreena.

Mom tried to explain why she had sent me to live with my dad. "I just couldn't support you on my own," she said. But after years of heartache, I wasn't in a forgiving mood. One night, lying in bed, Coreena snuggled close to me. "Your mother went for a blood test today to see if she's a potential donor," she said. I arched my eyebrows. "She wanted to give you one of her kidneys, but she's not a match. She's A-positive and your records say that you're O-positive."

"That's right. I was tested when I went to work for the trucking company," I said. I looked at Coreena quizzically. "Why is she trying so hard to be a mother to me now? Why wasn't she there when I really needed her?"

"Well, you need her now," Coreena said softly.

"No, I don't," I snapped.

The day my first disability check arrived, we packed our things and moved back to Oklahoma. But life didn't get any better. Being hooked up three times a week to the dialysis machine was really getting to me. I missed the freedom I had hauling cross-country loads, nothing but horizons ahead of me, the schedule my own, and a real paycheck—not a government check—at the end of the week.

Inside, frustration was building up like a toxin, but there was no cleansing dialysis. More and more I shouted at the girls when their playing annoyed me. When Coreena closed the door, saying we needed to talk, I turned my back. I spent most days in my bedroom, alone. I'd never felt so miserable. And my resentment toward my mom grew and grew. I was dying inside.

Now and then one of my daughters would try to rouse me. "Please, Daddy, come to church with us today," Joy, my seven-year-old, begged one Sunday.

"Not today," I said, burrowing under the blanket.

Joy didn't move. She stared at me, disappointment clouding her eyes. And disapproval. I saw a hard flash of it, my own child disapproving of me, her father. I remembered the vow I'd once made. That no one would be a better family man than I would be. That nothing would get in the way of my being a good dad. I was so full of bitterness I had stopped caring for my own family. It wasn't just my kidneys that needed healing. I got out of bed and got dressed.

I hadn't been to church much lately. Not nearly enough. I tried to focus on the minister's sermon. One word kept jumping out: forgiveness. *Not my strongest suit,* I thought. Yet, it seemed as if he were talking directly to me, stripping my bitterness bare for me to see. I'd been angry for so long. At my mother, about my illness. It was poisoning my relationship with my wife and children. I dropped my head and whispered, *Dear God, free me from this poison of anger. I don't want to live—or die—a bitter man. Please help me.*

That night my mother called. "Tell her . . ." I started to say to Coreena. I stopped myself. "Give me the phone, please," I said. We talked for a while. The words didn't come easy, as if I were literally choking on my feelings. But it was a start, maybe.

We talked a little more. And more, over the coming weeks and months. I didn't fully trust her. *After all, I* thought, *what has she ever really done for me?* I couldn't quite forgive her yet either, but maybe if I kept trying, maybe at least God would help me to have the desire to forgive even if it took the rest of my life.

I was in the hospital to have an access point inserted into my leg for dialysis when something went terribly wrong. A vein in my leg ruptured. I lost a great deal of blood and was rushed into surgery.

Some hours later I drifted back to consciousness. I was in a hospital bed. Above me, a bag of blood dripped intravenously into my arm. I stared at the bag. It said type A-positive. Anxiety shot through me. I punched the help button on my bed and yelled for a nurse. "That bag says A-positive!" I shouted. "My blood type is O-positive."

The nurse disconnected the tubing and checked my

vital signs. Then she checked the paperwork at the foot of my bed. "It says your blood type is A-positive, right here," she said, pointing to the chart.

"Impossible. When I started driving trucks at eighteen, I had a complete physical and they marked me as O-positive," I said. "It's a regular thing in case you're in an accident."

The nurse took a new blood sample from me. The results came back A-positive. There was another person in my family with the same blood type: my mother. Coreena called her before I could say anything.

As soon as Mom got off the phone she climbed into her car and made the five-hour drive to the hospital.

"I'm a match," she said, after taking a battery of tests. "Steve, I'm going to give you one of my kidneys." Her eyes were both pleading and defiant. Pleading for forgiveness, yet defiant of my anger as if to say how dare a son hate his mother.

And all at once I felt a whirlwind of emotions, of everything I'd been feeling for all these years. What was this emotion? A voice seemed to answer: *Forgive her.*

"Mom," I said, and took her hand and held it tightly for a long time.

Of course there could be a reason why my blood type suddenly seemed to change. A clerical error or maybe a mistake when I had my physical. A logical explanation. But the real miracle was the miracle of reconciliation. I couldn't have engineered that change of heart on my own.

After the transplant, Mom and I were given rooms on the same floor. Those first few days I was weak and sick from the anti-rejection drugs. Hour after hour Mom sat beside me, ignoring her own pain to be with me.

One time I awoke to find her standing by my bedside. I smiled at her. "Thank you," I said.

"Any mother would have done the same," she said, reaching for my hand.

No, not any mom, but my mother who gave me life not once but twice.

Chapter 4

Receiving Peace

I leave you peace; my peace I give you . . . So don't let your hearts be troubled or afraid (John 14:27 NCV).

Have you ever noticed how much easier it sometimes is to forgive others than to forgive yourself? Even when people we've hurt willingly accept our apologies and extend warm hands of forgiveness, we often still feel badly for what we did and continue to beat ourselves up over it. A great reward of truly *receiving* forgiveness when it's offered is a quieting, calming peace—the gift of God for a tender, repentant heart.

A Cry in the Night

MARY BELOTE

I'd slid into a shallow sleep that balmy spring night in 1993 when Matthew's fitful moans and cries awoke me, as they had nearly every night for five years. I got up from the mattress on the floor next to my six-year-old's bed and went to his side. "Shh, sweetie," I whispered, gathering him up in my arms. "Mommy's here."

Sinking down on my mattress again, I cradled Matthew on my lap and began rocking him. He had suffered massive brain damage at the age of seventeen months and since then things that used to be no problem, like getting him to stop crying, had become impossible. Life had turned into a never-ending struggle for me. I'd even begun seeing a psychologist, but trying to both take care of Matthew's needs and keep things going as smoothly as possible for my husband, Tom, and our three-year-old, Rebecca, I was utterly spent. *Lord, I am so tired of feeling like this. But how else can I go on?*

Even more than from sheer physical exhaustion, I was worn out from the strain of keeping up the front that had everyone—Matthew's doctors, neighbors, people from church—marveling at how well I seemed to cope. They didn't know that I had to do everything right for my husband and children to make up for that terrible time when I'd done everything wrong. Even though Tom and I referred to what had happened to our son as an accident, I knew it was my fault that Matthew's life— and ours—would never be the same again.

After all, I was the one who, in the flurry of packing for our trip back stateside after Tom's army tour of duty in Cameroon, had tucked the envelope containing our anti-malarial medication into my carry-on, Matthew's diaper bag. I was the one who had neglected to transfer those chloroquine pills into a childproof bottle once we were back in the States. I was the one who'd stepped into the kitchen that morning, January 20, 1988, and left Matthew alone in the living room—only briefly, but long enough for him to tip over the diaper bag and swallow the candylike pink pills that spilled out. And I was the one who had wasted precious minutes looking for ipecac to empty his stomach with, before finally heading to the hospital.

As I pulled up to the emergency room, Matthew started strangling. I snatched him up and tore inside. The ER staff kept me away from Matthew while they worked to revive him, but if he could hear anything, he would've heard my cries. The minutes seemed like hours as I pleaded with God. At last a doctor told me, "He's unconscious, but we've got him breathing again. We're moving him to

Children's Hospital. They're better equipped." The only thing that registered was, Matthew's breathing. He's alive!

Matthew was admitted to the intensive care unit at Children's that evening. The next day a doctor took Tom and me aside. "Your son's brain was deprived of oxygen for more than an hour," he explained. "I'm afraid the damage was severe." Tom's hand tightened around mine as the doctor went on. "We'll know more after we do some CAT scans."

How could I have let this happen to my son? I thought. *God, tell me what I can do for him now.*

Trust him to Me. I understand your pain.

Yielding to God was difficult. I was Matthew's mother. It was my job to be with him always, to protect him. My responsibility.

For weeks, I hardly left his side, talking to him, hoping he could hear me. Tom begged me to get some rest. I didn't listen to him any more than I'd listened to God. I wanted to stay with Matthew so he would see my face as he regained awareness. But the lack of any improvement in his condition, the repeated tests and the doctors murmuring "massive brain damage" scared me. Finally I dared to ask a neurologist, "Is this the way Matthew's going to be for the rest of his life?"

The doctor's sober expression confirmed my worst fears. "There won't be much change in his condition," he said. Tom and I had been so thrilled that Matthew had started walking and talking early, but the doctor explained he would never again be able to do either. His mental development wouldn't progress beyond the infant stage. He would be wheelchair-bound for as long as he lived. Though he wasn't completely paralyzed, he couldn't control body movements or functions. He would have to be fed through a tube in his stomach. His eyes, those inquisitive blue eyes that used to take in everything around him, could no longer see anything but light and dark.

The doctor's words sank in as I watched Matthew lie totally unresponsive in his hospital bed. Our bright, active little boy would remain trapped in body and mind forever. And I'm the one who did this to him. Me. I took his limp hand in my own. "I love you, Matthew, and I will never let you down again."

That spring, when Matthew's condition stabilized, we brought him to our new home in Washington, D.C., where Tom was now stationed. I threw myself into all the daily tasks of caring for my son. Bathing and dressing him. Changing his diapers. Pouring liquid meals into his feeding tube. Exercising his limbs. Even if it meant pushing myself to the point of collapse, living for Matthew was the only way I could live with myself.

What I couldn't bring myself to do was to talk about what had happened. Not to our neighbors or people at church (we never told them the details of Matthew's "accident"). Not even to Tom, despite how well we worked together to coordinate our son's care. Sometimes I caught a faraway look in Tom's eye when he saw boys Matthew's age playing, and I worried that I'd ruined his life too.

The only thing Matthew seemed able to do was cry—all day and all night. I spent hours and hours rocking him. Eventually his sobs quieted, but was it because of exhaustion rather than a real response to me? *Please, God,* I'd pray, holding Matthew, *let my son know I'm here for him. Let him know I love him.* God assured me He loved Matthew even more than I did.

Still, there was never any indication that Matthew was cognizant of anything outside himself. When Mother's Day came that year, Tom wanted to go out, but I didn't feel up to it. Instead I lay in bed cuddling Matthew. *What right do I have to celebrate this day?* I thought, stroking his thick blond hair.

Suddenly a delighted smile crossed Matthew's face, just like when I used to hold him before the accident. He recognizes my touch!

I became pregnant with my second child, and the added strain wore me down. The joy of Rebecca's birth in May 1989 was quickly overshadowed by the knowledge that one day I'd have to tell her what had happened to her brother and face her doubts about me as a mother. Looking after both kids left me in a state of constant exhaustion, which was made all the worse because I wouldn't allow it to show. If people saw how tired I was, they'd ask why I set such punishing demands on myself. How could I explain to them it was penance for what I'd done to my own son?

So I hid my guilt behind a facade of competence and control. I arrived at appointments with Matthew's doctors, social workers and teachers, impeccably dressed and well-versed in the latest innovations for kids with special needs. One program was a summer camp run by Joni Eareckson Tada that we went to in 1991. Tom and Rebecca enjoyed themselves, and even I relaxed enough to admit it was good to see how other families were coping.

Then one evening the man behind us in the buffet line said, "You must be the folks whose son took the medicine."

I froze. A pastor we'd confided in must have shared our story. As Tom and the man started talking, I excused myself and fled to our cabin. Later Tom found me. "Sooner or later, we'll have to tell people," he said quietly. "We'll have to tell Rebecca." He was right, but for the rest of our stay, I couldn't look anyone in the eye. They knew. And I was sure they were staring at me, judging me.

I was relieved to get home, where I buried myself in my usual routine. Tom and I began getting the kids together after dinner for a little family time. Mostly we'd sing songs they were learning in Sunday school. That always seemed to bring a smile to Matthew's face.

One evening Tom, Rebecca and I had just launched

into that week's selection, "Jesus Loves Me," when Matthew shifted restlessly in my lap. "What's the matter, sweetie?" I asked. The next thing I knew, he wasn't just smiling—he was laughing!

That breakthrough gave me the strength to tell Rebecca the truth. She was three, about to enter nursery school, and being around other kids would get her wondering about her brother. "There's something I want you to know," I said to her one day. "Matthew wasn't always this way." She glanced at her brother in his wheelchair and turned back to me, puzzled. "He used to walk and talk just like you. Then Mommy left some medicine out by mistake. Matthew took it, and it made him sick. That's why he's different now."

Gazing at me trustingly, Rebecca nodded. "Okay, Mommy." I let out a breath I hadn't even been aware I was holding. And for the first time since the accident, I allowed myself to think, *Maybe I don't have to be afraid of people judging me anymore. Maybe life will be different.*

It didn't take long for my hopes to be dimmed. One afternoon Rebecca came home from school and asked wistfully, "Mommy, when will I have a brother who can play with me?"

My guilt surged through me uncontrollably. I'd deprived Matthew of a life with meaning; Tom, of a son who could follow in his footsteps; Rebecca, of a big brother who could play with her.

I started seeing a psychologist. But in the dark of night, when Matthew cried out, unable to sleep as he was unable to do so many things, guilt and despair swept over me until they finally overwhelmed me.

That balmy spring night in 1993, when Matthew's fitful moans and cries awoke me for the thousandth time, I huddled on my mattress with my son and gave in at last. My arms weary from rocking Matthew, I broke down and admitted to God what I couldn't admit to anyone else. "Lord, I can't live like this anymore. But how else can I go on?"

Let go of the past, and trust Me.

"I'll try," I promised just as a breeze whispered through the window, ruffling Matthew's hair. He sighed once and fell silent, asleep again. My arms relaxed, and I sensed a small yet unmistakable release of the guilt I'd held onto as tightly as I held onto my son.

That was the beginning. A few months later, I summoned up the courage to have a long-overdue talk with Tom. I asked him to forgive me for hurting our son and making our lives so difficult.

"Of course," Tom said. But in my soul I couldn't bring myself to accept his forgiveness.

Tom wanted to start a disabilities-awareness group at our church. "I'll be telling the congregation about Matthew," he said. "Do you think you might be ready for that now?"

I nodded, remembering my promise to God.

The Sunday Tom spoke, other moms came up to me afterward. One told me about her son nearly drowning in their pool. Another said her daughter accidentally took a whole bottle of Tylenol. Still I kept thinking, *But they handled it well. Their kids are fine now.*

Later when I talked to my therapist about it, I admitted, "They wanted to sympathize, but I wouldn't let them. I don't know why I think no one can understand how I feel." I began attending a support group he recommended. At one meeting, the leader made an observation: "Sometimes life's hardest when people choose to take control rather than taking God's forgiveness."

She hadn't been talking to me specifically, and yet that statement stayed with me for weeks. I knew God was trying to tell me something.

One Sunday at church someone had the children sing "Jesus Loves Me." As their music filled the sanctuary, Matthew tossed his head back and laughed.

Look how happy he is.

Yes, he was happy right then. And even amid the difficulties of the years since the accident, the struggles I had been through with Matthew, hadn't there been other moments like that? Hadn't my deepest prayers for my son been answered? His smiles told me that he knew my love; his laughter, that he knew God's.

Finally Forgiven

MARIE HAWS

We were playing mini-golf, my friend and I, but we'd gotten together that afternoon mostly to talk. Girl stuff, like clothes and guys and who was seen with whom at the movies. Definitely private conversation and not to be shared with anyone. So when I noticed a young boy hovering behind us at the second hole, and then again at the third, I ignored him. "He's all by himself, poor kid," I said to my friend, suspecting he wanted to join our game.

Sure enough, at the fourth hole, the one with the red windmill that always blocked my ball, there he was. The boy managed a shy smile.

"Will you play with me?" he asked.

Leaning on my club, I looked down at him with my most adult frown. "No," I said. "Absolutely not."

The boy was crushed. I could see it in his face, almost as if I had slapped him. He dropped his club and hurried away, disappearing into the crowd.

What had I done? My friend lowered her eyes. My behavior was unforgivable, and I knew it. Only then did

I realize how much courage it must have taken for the boy to approach us, given we were so much older than he was.

For years afterward I kept wanting to call the boy back, to call the moment back and have another chance. How could I have been so selfish?

One day last summer I awoke with that memory weighing on my mind. That afternoon I even e-mailed a friend to say how much it still troubled me. "It's the one thing I can never forgive myself for," I confessed.

Coming home from the store at sundown I spotted a hand waving at me across a white picket fence. It was the woman who owned the house on the corner, out tending her rose garden. We'd chatted in passing, but with my work schedule I wasn't around much in the daytime.

"Hello!" I called.

At that moment, the woman's little boy scrambled through the gate and came rushing toward me. He flung himself at me with all his strength, wrapping his arms around my legs. "Will you play with me?" he asked.

Suddenly I was back to that day years ago at the mini-golf course. I looked into this neighbor boy's face and said, "Sure!"

He rushed to the fence where his mother stood and grabbed a blue Frisbee. He laughed and laughed as we chased the disk up and down the sidewalk.

"Thank you for playing with me," the boy said, the twilight casting a halo around his deep-gold hair.

"I'll remember it forever," I promised. He and his mother headed inside, and I practically floated down the street toward home, the burden of that unhappy memory lifted at last.

An Old Rotary Dial Telephone

NANCY B. GIBBS

Several years ago, I met a lady whom I admired not only for her radiant smile and heartwarming demeanor, but also for her ability to forgive. One quiet afternoon she shared her story with me. Before she finished telling me the details of an afternoon she had never forgotten, tears were streaming down my face. Her story went like this.

"I could never part with this old rotary dial telephone." She picked the telephone up and held it close to her heart. "It may be old and outdated but it saved my life."

"The day started out like every other day. I was busy working around my house when I heard a knock on my door. When I opened it, a young man pushed his way inside my home and physically attacked me. The pain was excruciating. He beat me unmercifully and dragged me into another room. My ankles were broken. I couldn't count the bruises or cuts that I endured. It was a miracle that I lived."

My friend told me how she heard a voice during the attack. "Just play dead," the voice echoed in her ears. "He won't stop hitting you until he thinks you are dead—so play dead." She told me how after she heard the voice she stayed as still as possible, even though she was in an incredible amount of pain. She watched the young man go through her belongings until he found her purse. He stuck her purse under his arm and raced out the front door. She heard the door slam behind him.

Once he was gone, my friend was able to drag her bruised and battered body over to the telephone. She called the police. In just a few minutes, help arrived. Oddly, the young man was sitting on the curb in front of her house rambling through her purse. He was arrested on the spot.

An ambulance took my friend to a nearby hospital where she stayed for several weeks. It took her a long time to recover well enough to be able to return home. When she returned home, however, she moved to a smaller assisted-living apartment complex. There she would feel safe as she knew there were those who would be watching out for her.

After intense and painful therapy, my friend learned to walk again. She seldom walked without pain, however. The horror of that afternoon would live with her forever.

So she would save the telephone that saved her life.

My friend had every right to become bitter and show her anger toward this young man who was spending time in jail. Instead of carrying anger toward him, however, she forgave him. He never asked for her forgiveness, but she knew that if she wanted to exemplify Christ, she had to ask herself what Jesus would have done in the same situation.

In addition to forgiving the young man, she began praying for him on a daily basis. She told me that each morning she asked God to bless him and to forgive him for the injustice he had done to her. And every time her ankles hurt, she talked to God about showing mercy toward the angry young man. Every time the rotary style telephone rang, she felt a sense of gratitude as she remembered how God spared her.

Several months later, she was asked about testifying against the young man in court. She didn't want to, but agreed, only if it was absolutely necessary for justice to be done. While she wanted to forgive him, she didn't want the same thing to happen to someone else. God was merciful, however, and the case was tried without her testimony. She thanked God oftentimes for his mercy in that situation.

I was amazed at how this woman of God could forgive a person for the severe injustice he committed toward her. But she proved it could be done. And, in addition, she never lost her smile. Her joy showed through every situation she endured. She loved the Lord regardless of the difficulties that came her way.

Several years later, an illness invaded her life. My friend knew her time here on earth was short. She looked to me for support and love. I was like a child to her, even though we had only known each other for a few short years. When she whispered her last good-bye to me, she was more concerned about me than herself.

"Are you going to be okay?" she asked, as tears fell down her cheek. "I'm worried about you."

"I'll be fine, but I will miss you so badly," I answered. I realized that I would miss many things about this incredible lady. I would miss her smile, her joy for living and her willingness to do anything she could for other people. But mostly I would miss experiencing her forgiving spirit.

I wanted to beg her to not leave me, but I knew it was impossible for her to stay. So I just held her close and made some important promises to her. I would try to carry on her legacy and be as kind to other people as she was. I would learn to forgive as she forgave and as God forgives—as far as the east is to the west. I would never forget her. I also promised her that I would look for her as I step through the gates of heaven myself someday.

Following my friend's death, my grown son said that the saddest part of her passing was that there was one less person left here on earth like her. She was one of a kind and possessed a heart of gold.

The day her apartment was being emptied, I picked up the old telephone. "Take good care of this," I told her niece. "This telephone saved her life."

It's been six years since my friend's death. But when I become impatient with someone or get aggravated about the injustice others pour upon me, I think of her and remember the promises I made to her and to myself.

My friend's legacy still lingers in my heart and soul today. I still remember the sincerity in her voice the day she held the telephone close to her heart and told me how it saved her life. I oftentimes think of her lively attitude even right up until the day she went to be with the Lord.

I pray that when it is my time to leave this world behind that I can break through the clouds, just as she did, with no regrets. I also pray that I won't be carrying an unforgiving attitude toward any person that I leave behind, regardless of what they may have done to me. Being able to forgive those who seem unforgivable has to be a miracle from God.

Freed from Rage

PHYLLIS DOMINGUEZ

I'd just come home from dropping my daughter off at her high school when I noticed the light flashing on the answering machine. The message was from one of the nurses at my mother's assisted-living center. "You need to come over," she said. "Your mother won't leave her apartment, not even to eat. We don't know what to do with her."

God, give me strength, I asked as I turned and headed back out the door. Like the nurses, I sometimes didn't know what do about my mother either. In her eighties, weakened by diabetes and pneumonia and ever-deepening dementia, she was unpredictable and difficult.

And the situation this morning, I was informed when I got to the center, was much worse than usual. They'd tried to coax Mother into the dining room, but she'd erupted into a rage—screaming, cursing, lashing out at anyone who came near.

The nurses were shocked but I wasn't. I'd known that rage when I was a small girl. I had felt her belt raising welts on my legs and heard the curses that hurt even

156

more. "It's your fault," she'd say. "If you were good, Mama wouldn't lose her temper." By the time I was seven, I had promised myself I wouldn't be anything at all like my mother.

Growing up, I had lived day to day trying to steer clear of the fighting between Daddy and Mother, and the anger she sometimes took out on me. I would shut myself away in my room and play the French horn for hours, letting the music drown out the cursing and shouting.

After my parents' divorce, Mother did work hard to support us, but there wasn't money for me to go away to college. I arranged for my own tuition and commuted to a local university. Mother had always encouraged me to get a good education, and somehow she managed to buy me a horn when I decided to major in music. But as soon as I earned my degree, I moved out.

I made my own life—a happy one with Mike, the wise and gentle man who became my husband, and Mary, our daughter. I made sure Mary knew how much I loved her. "We're proud of you," I'd tell her so often that she finally asked me to stop.

We saw Mother from time to time, mostly during the holidays. The one thing she and I could agree on was Mary. It was plain to see Mother adored her only grandchild. Except for those occasional visits, though, I kept my distance. It was easier not to think about the pain of my past that way, easier to believe I was free of my mother.

Then her health began its slow collapse, and I was dragged back into her life. When the trips to the hospital were necessary and the calls from the assisted-living center came, I felt trapped. I resented having to drop whatever I was doing and go to her. Like this morning.

Stepping inside Mother's apartment, I could tell she had driven off the staff. The air smelled like dirty laundry. The hamper and wastebaskets were overflowing. Mother slumped in her recliner, still in her bathrobe. "Go away!" she shrieked.

I wished I could. I'd prayed, sought spiritual counsel. I'd read the scriptures, looking for loopholes, but the rules hadn't changed: "Honor thy father and thy mother . . . "

"Mother," I said, "you need to get dressed."

"I won't!"

"You need to dress," I repeated, "so you can go to the dining room."

"What dining room?"

"The dining room down the hall. It's where you eat."

"No, I don't. Go away! Stop it!"

"You stop it now!" I remembered Mother yelling at me when I was little. "Stop crying, or I'll punish you some more." I would choke down the tears, only to feel a terrible fire deep inside that I later learned was rage. "You think you got it bad?" I could remember her shouting at me when I was a teenager. "Try growing up like I did, the daughter of the town drunk!" Even knowing her tragic past didn't change the way I felt about her now. Who could tell how she was going to mess up my life next? I wanted none of it.

Mother's voice came again, plaintive now. "I wish you'd talk to me."

Honor thy father and thy mother.

At least it said honor and not love.

I walked into the bedroom, picked up a housedress and took it back to where my mother was sitting. "Come on," I said. "Let's get dressed."

"Why?" She scowled at me.

"So you can go eat."

"I'm not going anywhere."

"You have to eat. You're diabetic." I draped the dress over my arm and bent over her recliner. "I'll help you up."

She spat a profanity.

I ignored it. "Come on, Mama, let's get up."

Then she did it. She hit me. My head, my arm.

I stepped back, stunned. I felt the dress underfoot. I must have dropped it.

Time seemed to slow. I stood there, staring at my mother, something terrible building inside me.

Go on. Hit her. Now's your chance.

I could do it, could get my revenge. Finally hurt Mother the way she'd hurt me. Show her what it felt like, all those times when I couldn't fight back.

She's got it coming.

My arm trembled. All those times . . .

But if I hit her, would anything be better? Hadn't there been enough hurting? It had to stop here. Somehow I would have to let go of this rage and bitterness and let God help me bear it.

I forced myself to reach down and pick up the dress. "Let's put this on," I said.

I felt a sudden shift, a change, something like motion— in the room at first, then in my body. A peculiar warmth filled me, gentle as a soft light.

What's happening? I thought.

The warmth grew stronger, and with it a tremendous sense of freedom. Of forgiveness.

I looked at Mother, huddled in her recliner. For the first time, I saw her without the blinders of my own anger. She was only an old lady, frail and helpless. I eased her up out of her chair and got her into her dress.

No outpouring of love for my mother followed. Not then and not when I went to help her in the months that came after. But I found that the rage and pain I'd carried with me for years had lifted, never to return. A little at a time, sadness, then understanding, took their place, and that was better.

In the autumn of 1999, Mother fell and broke a hip, and she died a short time later. I wept for her. I saw how she had been worn down by struggling to overcome her own childhood suffering, a violent and troubled marriage and the ravages of dementia.

I mourned for the lost love between us, the love that I had longed for. I realized that she had tried to reach out to me over the years—especially when it came to my education and my music—and I believe that in her way, my mother longed for that same love too.

I wrote her obituary. "She worked hard all her life," it read in part. I mentioned how she'd passed her love of books and learning on to me. I wanted people to know the best about her.

Honor thy mother.

Only God could have given me the forgiveness and freedom I needed to finally say that I do.

In His Perfect Time

CARLA M. ZWAHLEN

I think you are adrenaline deprived," said my niece, while she swept up the flower debris strewn around the floor. We were cleaning up after designing and installing the flowers for my client's three hundred-guest wedding extravaganza. Adrenaline deprived or whatever it was, I ran on empty. It was a hot early evening in August 2004. This wedding project was the first major job I had accepted since my husband, Werner, lost his heroic battle against esophageal cancer in June of 2003.

Werner's death severed the roots of my life. Like a shocked plant, I barely functioned. To begin the severe work of walking through mind numbing grief, I needed a quiet refuge. That priceless gift of time came from a prince and princess, who offered me a place of refuge at their secluded ancestral chateau in the heart of France.

My sister manages this French prince's international business affairs. In the winter of 2004, her job required her to travel to his chateau, in order to work on an extended major project. When the prince found out about Werner's death, he extended a kind and gracious invitation to me to accompany my sister, and stay at the chateau for as long as I needed. Because nothing about living in a palace environment was familiar to me, and nothing there existed of the life I shared with Werner, the chateau became my perfect refuge.

The mild winter climate in the French region was also a gift. Almost everday, I walked through formal boxwood gardens and into the solitude of the manicured forest surrounding the chateau. I did not walk alone. I had God's promise to rest in His shadow as we walked through the steps of mourning. I deliberately sought His purpose and plan to help me begin my life again when I returned home to New Hampshire in April. One major decision loomed over the rest. Could I continue to live in the home Werner and I shared for thirty-three years? I should not have worried. On the day I returned to my home God knew best how to handle that decision.

On a warm April afternoon, I walked into my home and burst into tears. Werner would never return to this house, and I could not find or recapture my old life there. That abrupt reality and emotional explosion solidified the impossibility of living in my home without Werner. To help calm me, my daughter-in-law took me aside and gave me a glass of water. As I drank the water, I said, "I can't do this. I can't live here." A few months later, I placed my house on the market. The completion of this huge August wedding project marked the last chapter of living in my home.

Alone in my house later that night I finally sank into a chair. My thoughts roved back over the day's wedding work. Then my throughts tread on shaky ground. *Werner, you would have been proud of the work we accomplished and how exquisite the flowers looked in the grand ballroom.* I should have known better. His silent voice roared around me. I crashed.

Grief never asked permission to visit me. It just barged in like the suffocating wind of a tornado's vortex. It threw off a heavy shroud of longing for Werner and hung it on me. Grief never visited alone. It came with its entourage. One called *inconsolable* embraced me. One called *irrational desire* led me into the room of irrational thought. God knew nothing about commonsense. *If I see Werner one more time, I'll be OK. I'll look at his picture. His picture will console me.* I picked up his photograph and looked at it. His fixed smile and beautiful brown eyes stared back at me. I touched its flatness. He was now only a picture in the house. I slammed the picture face down on the table. It only increased my ache to hear his voice. I stretched out my hand to touch him somewhere in the beyond, but the beyond was out of my reach. Mocking my gesture, grief's entourage whispered those hated words, *He's gone, he's gone.* I sank back down into the chair and became unglued.

Somewhere in my mind a small voice said, *Fight back or this shroud of longing will suffocate you.* I grabbed a book from the table next to my chair and randomly opened it. *I'll read. Reading will get my focus back.* Two words on the top of the page read, "Everlasting Consolation." I stared at the words, wiped my tears and read on . . .

> Consolation—there is music in the word. Like David's harp, it charms away the evil spirit of melancholy. All earthborn consolations are fleeting in essence and short lived in their existence. They are brilliant and fragile as the rainbow hues of a soap bubble, but the consolation that God gives does not fade nor lose its freshness. It stands all tests, the shock of trial, the passing years, and death itself.

The next sentence held the weapon that loosed grief's grip on me: "Are you pining and refusing to be comforted? Is this honorable to God? Cheer up. Jesus gives eternal consolation." C.H. Spurgeon, *Evening by Evening.*

Perhaps, I said to the question. Perhaps consolation is not what I want. *Perhaps I want the prize I had, my husband.* As quickly as I responded to the question, the defense I often used against grief's onslaught came to mind. *If you allow even the impossibility of that thought to take a breath in your mind, Werner would suffer again, you would have to say good-bye to him again.* No, I never want him back here to make my life bearable. I slowly calmed down.

When I went to bed later that night, sleep eluded me. Emotionally exhausted from another walk in the fire of sorrow, I gave up the bed and knelt at my open window. The blackness magnified the star's brilliance. As I knelt under the millions of stars looking down at me, I thought of the other sleepless nights that sent me out of my bed and to the window for a midnight rendezvous with God.

One of those recurring dreams woke me. In the dream Werner stood near me, yet distant and silent. The other woman was there. She always was there. The woman I came to understand represented death. Werner was powerless to escape her beckoning. She always took him from me. The dream always woke me.

I climbed out from under the down covers of the antique sleigh bed, went to the tall heavy double windows, and pushed them wide open. The cool February night breeze brushed past me. The boxwood hedges and poplar trees surrounding the chateau stood like silhouetted sentinels against the sky. Magnificent infinite indigo touched the rolling hills of the French countryside's horizon.

The night sky became my sanctuary and the windowsill my altar. It brought me closer to heaven's door, where I had an interest. I always imagined God standing in the doorway, and beside Him stood Werner, perfect and healed.

Sophistication is not a needy child's requirement. "God," I said, "I just need to know you are here. Send a shooting star so that I know you hear me." I felt silly to make such a childish request. Moments later, my eyes grew big like a child who received an unexpected gift.

A star shot out across the dark sky, followed right behind by another star. Down they fell together and disappeared into the night. I guess I forgot I was a child of God. He didn't. He breathed His consolation across the heavens and blew two stars out of place to reassure me of His presence.

In April I left France and traveled to Switzerland where I spent a few weeks with Werner's family, who were very special to me. However, I had a love/hate relationship with being in Switzerland. Everything Swiss spoke of Werner. Everywhere I went the presence of his absence accompanies me as a constant reminder of the remnant of our marriage.

One night, before I traveled up into the Alps to the village where Werner was born, and where we were married, a flood of memories sent sleep flying from me and sent me fleeing to my bedroom window, where I sought God's protection against grief's imminent attack.

I opened the long windows above my bed, but the night wind rushed into the room too cold for me to rest my elbows on the windowsill. I left the windows wide open, and I slipped back under the down quilt. Under the night sky that became my canopy, I wrestled with the painful and difficult challenges tomorrow's journey presented. I asked God to let me go forward under His arms of support and courage.

I must walk to the churchyard where thirty-three years ago the laughter of family and friends filled the air, and all the church bells joyously rang out across the valley to celebrate our wedding day. A few months ago I walked with my family to that same churchyard. We walked to the cemetery under the awful toll of a lone bell's drone across the valley.

Tomorrow I cannot take that walk to Werner's grave for the first time since his burial in my own strength. Help me tonight to get through this unbearable anticipation by sending a . . . I stopped.

He is not your magician, I reminded myself. However, my distress wasn't insignificant to God. His ways are not dependent on my temporal view of Him.

There it came—a brilliant lone star fell down the night sky, sent, in perfect time, to prepare me to walk on in His strength. Once again, He spread His rod and staff across the heavens to comfort me.

As I knelt at my bedroom window, after this long August day of wedding work, I realized during the past year I had traveled many miles physically, emotionally, and spiritually. I recalled the times despair pushed me to the end of my coping skills, God reached down and scooped me up in His everlasting arms of comfort. In the midst of my darkest nights, He set the stars in motion to light my path. The warm August air settled quietly on my flesh. God's breath of peace settled softly around my spirit.

In a few weeks I face a new transition. Life will begin over again in a new home. I know You will prepare the way. I spoke to Him up to where a few stars struggled to shine out from the darkest place in the sky.

All of a sudden a brilliant triangle banner of sizzling yellows burst out of that darkness and flew across space like a mini firework. *Wow!* I said. Was my meteor display a coincidence? Who cares? God cared enough to place me at the window in His perfect time.

I knelt by the window a while longer. Awe and humble gratitude kept me there. *Not once, not twice, but three times,* I thought, *the God of the universe, sent down His heavenly night messengers to lift me out of the valley of grief's grip.*

The stars, like the soap bubbles, were short-lived. However, unlike the soap bubbles blown up by human breath, God made the shooting stars. The words, "everlasting consolation" swept through me like a lullaby's soothing melody. I went to bed and slept.

My Trusted Friend

JOANNE K. HILL

My parents divorced when I was in first grade, and for several years I was shifted from home to home. Grandma Gladys became my refuge. To some, Grandma was not perfect, as she was prone to holding grudges. But for a lonely, sickly little girl, she was an angel. Most families I stayed with disliked taking care of me when I was sick; so I was often shuttled to Grandma's house. Sometimes I think I got sick just so I could stay with her.

After Mom remarried, I still spent time with Grandma, often staying over the weekend or for days at a time during the summer. Years later, I took my children to see her frequently, although she lived nearly an hour's drive away. She was my confidant, my mentor, and my friend.

When Grandma became unable to care for herself, I was the one who found a nursing facility and moved her into it. Her three children had promised never to do this, but none of them was in a position to care for a woman with Alzheimer's disease. Something had to be done, as Grandma was found wandering in her nightgown in the middle of the night.

Whenever I visited Grandma, she talked about me as though I weren't there.

"Joanne came one day and drove me around in circles. Then she dumped me here," she told my granddaughter one day.

I choked back a cry, knowing Grandma was telling me she was angry with me. Although I knew that she now was on good terms with all her children, it still hurt. She thought I was trying to shut her away. How I wished I could care for her as she had for me! When we tried that arrangement, however, it had not worked. Frequent visits to the nursing home assured me that she was safe and well cared for.

As the years went by, however, my resolve to be there for Grandma weakened. My visits grew fewer and shorter. The day I received a phone call notifying me that Grandma had pneumonia and was dying, shame filled my heart. I recalled my last visit, a whole year before.

That hot, humid day I had gone to the nursing home in response to a similar call, certain my love was strong enough to let her go. When I entered the room, Grandma lay in bed, curled up like a newborn baby. Her snow-white hair fanned the pristine pillowcase. Grandma's eyes were closed, her breathing labored. Nurses had attempted to make her comfortable, but Grandma remained tense, her face drawn into a frown.

As I leaned down to kiss Grandma Gladys's sunken

cheeks, I whispered, "Grandma. Grandma, it's Joanne. Remember me?"

She showed no signs of recognition. As I gently stroked her shriveled body, I thought of the times when my beautiful grandmother had offered a soft lap to climb into, a bosom on which to lay my head. I recalled the many times she dried my tears, and wiped a feverish brow. Now the arms that held me were black and blue from thrashing around as her soul sought to escape a worn-out body.

A nurse pulled a chair next to the bed, and I sat down.

"Grandma, it's Joanne," I said again, taking her hand in mine. "I'm here. Don't be afraid. I love you." Grandma did not open her eyes, but she seemed to relax a little.

Dear God help me, I prayed silently. *Oh, God. This is so hard. How can I say good-bye? I know she's in pain, but she's been my best friend.* I drew in a deep breath. *Yet, I don't want her to suffer anymore.* I held her hand for hours, it seemed.

"Grandma, it's okay," I finally managed. "You can go now if you want. I love you."

Grandma's hand relaxed in mine, and her breathing became shallow. Then it happened. I panicked. With a cry I dropped Grandma's hand and fled. All the way home, angry tears coursed down my cheeks.

Ashamed at not being able to stay with Grandma during her time of need, I did not return. Yet the fact that she still lay imprisoned within her body weighed heavily upon my heart. Now, a year later, another phone call brought back all those feelings. *I cannot do this. I will not go,* I told myself.

One day passed, then two. On the third day, I set out to run some errands. Suddenly I realized I was driving toward the nursing home. My heart pounded. My driving mirrored my indecision as I slowed down, sped up, then slowed down again.

"Oh God, help me stay this time," I prayed aloud. As if in answer, a voice sang from the radio: "Good-bye to you, my trusted friend." The words convinced me I was headed in the right direction.

When I saw the raised bedside bars and Grandma's thrashing body, I prayed silently once again. *I need you, Lord. Please help me do this.*

A nurse sat nearby as I approached Grandma's bed. Tears stung my eyes as I searched for the right words.

"May I put down the side so I can get closer to her?" I asked. The nurse rose, put down the safety rail, then pulled the chair up close for me and left the room.

I brushed Grandma's beautiful snow-white hair off her troubled face, then whispered, "I love you, Grandma," and kissed her forehead. Gently, I took one of her hands into mine as I sat down. Although she still thrashed, she did not pull her hand from mine.

"Remember how you used to rub my back? Remember how we slept spoon fashion in bed on cold winter nights?"

Grandma's thrashing slowed a bit.

"Remember how I came over to wash your collection of salt-and-pepper shakers? How you helped the other kids and me put on circuses and plays in your backyard?"

With each question, Grandma grew calmer, but the panic from the year before reared its ugly head. I tightly shut my eyes and prayed fervently for help. With amazing clarity, I detected the source of my grandmother's agony—unresolved forgiveness—and knew what I was to do.

"It's okay, Grandma. God forgives you. I forgive you, and I believe you forgive me. I know you forgive your sister, Mazie, also." One by one, I listed people from the past who had hurt or been hurt by Grandma.

"Grandma, you are forgiven. Everyone forgives you. Everyone accepts your forgiveness." With those words, release came for both of us. The calm I had felt briefly the year before returned, and Grandma quietly stretched out her frail body. Peace relaxed her face. It was as though we were both suspended in time with no regrets and no fears.

Even when Grandma's breathing quieted, I didn't move away. We continued to hold hands in silence.

Some time passed before I noticed music in the room. The same voice I'd heard earlier on the car radio sang, "Good-bye to you, my trusted friend."

A glowing smile covered Grandma's face. Her breathing, once labored, grew slow and easy.

I closed my eyes and said a prayer of thanks. When I opened them, the whole room seemed radiant. A row of nurses, all dressed in white, stood alongside the bed, quietly weeping. But they did not seem like tears of sadness.

"Say hello to Grandpa for me," I whispered as I kissed her good-bye.

I walked to my car, and within minutes of starting for home, the comforting song filled the car and my heart. "Good-bye to you, my trusted friend."

Grandma Gladys, still smiling, died two hours after I arrived home. Together, my trusted friend and I had walked through the valley of the shadow of death and found no evil.

Chapter 5

Redeeming the Lost

Jesus said, "I came to find lost people and save them"
(Luke 19:10 NCV adapted).

Forgiveness, in it's purest form, came to the world through Jesus, the Son of God. His sweet sacrifice gives us the divine healing touch of forgiveness without which we cannot live eternally. It is our great privilege and joy to model His love and forgiveness to others and participate in His divinely appointed mission on earth—redeeming the lost by reconciling them to the Father.

Forgiveness Brings Healing

CHUCK DEAN

The room suddenly grew silent. Every eye was fixed on me as I stood beside the speaker's lectern. A deep, gnarly feeling in the pit of my stomach told me to run and hide. I stayed planted, not because I was a courageous man, but because God had told me to say what I had just said. I remained in place only through His strength.

After speaking the unspeakable before a group of over two hundred Vietnam veterans, I read every emotion known to man on their faces. Some were shocked with unbelief; many wanted to take me outside, while others searched for reasons to leave the room.

In the course of teaching an anger management workshop, the Lord led me to tell this room full of warriors the unthinkable: I had forgiven a certain American actress for her gross misdeeds regarding the Vietnam War during the sixties and seventies, and I encouraged them to do the same.

After the initial assault on their sense of reality, they allowed me to continue without too much ruckus. Since I was also a Vietnam vet, they figured I deserved to be heard out before they strung me up.

I shared the story of God showing me the destructive personal consequences of harboring unforgiveness for someone who many consider to be a Vietnam-era betrayer of our country. I understood that as long as I couldn't forgive her, I was in relational bondage to her. God had spoken to my heart, "As long as you cannot forgive her, you'll have a spiritual relationship with her that doesn't please Me."

After asking the group for a show of hands of those who wanted to be free from this woman and what she represented to them, many hands shot into the air. As I prayed for these men's deliverance, the crash bars on the exit door banged open. I paused, looking up to see a big marine in his wheelchair hurriedly leave the room.

Rob had been a hard-charging marine in Vietnam until a machine-gun bullet caught him in the spine. He had been confined to a wheelchair for twenty years and accepted Christ as his Savior only a couple of weeks prior to the conference.

Seeing him flee the room, I suspected he was headed out to his car to get a gun. He told me later that the last thing he wanted to hear was a teaching about forgiving this person. Although he was a Christian now, there were still a lot of rough edges.

Thinking that Rob was disgusted with the idea of forgiving her, I shrugged off his quick departure and continued praying for the men who had raised their hands (most of the men in the room, by the way).

About an hour after the session, I was fellowshipping in the hallway with some of the men when we witnessed the surprise of our lives. Rob, who had not been out of his wheelchair for twenty years, walked in the door and marched straight into the cheering arms of the dozens of veterans who had just been freed from the soul bondage of unforgiveness.

When I asked Rob what happened, he said, "I decided to give in and prayed that God would help me to forgive that actress. When I said that prayer, my legs suddenly tingled with feeling. The sensation in my legs scared me so much that I went straight to the VA hospital to have them checked out. After probing around, they discovered that I had feeling in my legs. So I got up and walked out, leaving my wheelchair behind." Then, with obvious gratitude he added, "Not only am I free from her, but I'm free from my wheelchair too!"

Hearing Rob give his personal testimony several times after that unforgettable day, I noticed that he never put much emphasis on his miraculous ability to walk again. In fact, every time I heard him testify about his Christian conversion, I had to remind him to testify about God healing his back and legs as well.

You see, to Rob, a man who knew the wretchedness of life from the inside out, just the simple fact that God wanted to save him from the pit of hell was enough of a miracle to last him a lifetime.

The Dragon and
the Preacher

JOHNNY LEE CLARY

I first met Reverend Wade Watts when we were both asked to speak on a Tulsa radio program. He put out his hand and I stepped back, offended. I was the Grand Dragon of the Ku Klux Klan in Oklahoma, and he was the state president of the NAACP. There was no way you would catch me shaking hands with him.

My training in hate began early. I was five years old when my father encouraged me to lean out our car window and shout racial slurs as we passed a bus stop. Daddy grinned and patted me on the back. "That's my boy," he said. When I was older I sat up late at night listening to stories my Uncle Harold told about shooting at black men who crossed his property. Daddy and Uncle Harold would howl with laughter.

My grandmother, though, read to me from the Bible and prayed for me. Once, I came home from Sunday school singing a song I had learned: "Jesus loves the lit-

183

tle children, All the children of the world; Red and yellow, black and white, they are precious in His sight . . ."

"Don't ever let me catch you singing words like that again!" Daddy's voice thundered. That was the end of Sunday school for me.

One night when I was eleven, I came home and found Daddy standing with a gun to his head. As I watched in horror, he pulled the trigger. After the funeral, Mama sent me to California to live with my older sister and her boyfriend. Lonely and confused, I spent a lot of time staring at the TV, and one day I saw a talk-show host interviewing David Duke, the Grand Wizard of the Ku Klux Klan. Fascinated, I asked around about how to get in touch with the Klan, and before long a representative came to visit. "Son," he said, "what you need is a real family—the Klan."

Week after week he showed up to take me to meetings. Desperate to belong to something, at the age of fourteen I joined as a full-fledged member. Eventually I became David Duke's boydguard, and by the time I was twenty I had become the Grand Dragon of Oklahoma.

I was a tireless recruiter for the Klan in Oklahoma, and it grew under my leadership. I was a fiery speaker, spreading the gospel of hate. That's why when I was asked to speak at that particular radio station in Tulsa in 1979 I jumped at the chance. Only shortly before the program did I learn it would be a debate between the

NAACP's Reverend Wade Watts and me. But I wasn't worried. I looked forward to it—a chance to put a black man in his place.

So I refused to shake hands with the nicely dressed older gentleman carrying a worn Bible. But as I took in his strong, kind face and dignified manner, he reached out and shook my hand anyway. "Hello, Mr. Clary," he said. "I'm Reverend Watts. Before we go in, I just want you to know that I love you and Jesus loves you."

Our on-air debate went back and forth, me firing off reasons the races should never have anything to do with each other, and the Reverend politely refuting everything I said and quoting Scripture. When he zeroed in on me with pointed questions about the beliefs I held, I could only mumble the generic slogans of the Klan. I became flustered by his calm. "I'm not listening to any more," I snarled, storming out.

I gathered my things and was heading through the lobby when the reverend appeared. I would have gladly pushed him out of my way except that he was holding a baby in his arms. "Mr. Clary, this is my daughter, Tia," he said. "And I have one last question for you." He held out a little girl with shining dark eyes and skin, and one of the sweetest expressions I had ever seen. "You say you hate all black people, Mr. Clary. Just tell me—how can you hate this child?"

Stunned, I turned and almost ran. I heard the reverend call after me: "I'm going to love you and pray for you, Mr. Clary, whether you like it or not!"

I didn't like it. Over the next ten years I had two burning goals. One was to climb the Klan's national ranks to the position of Imperial Wizard. The second was to make Reverend Wade Watts pay for what he had done. I would make him hate me.

But as ferociously as the Oklahoma Klan continued its campaign, just as firmly Reverend Wade Watts worked for justice and equality. Klansmen barraged his family with threatening phone calls. His windows were broken; effigies were torched on his lawn. His church was burned to the ground. The thirteen Watts children— a number of whom were adopted—were threatened and had to be escorted to school by the highway patrol. Once or twice I found myself thinking about that baby, little Tia. I drove the thought away with hate. Still, nothing the Klan did stopped the reverend, nothing shut him up. When he joined ranks with an Oklahoma senator to outlaw the telephone hot lines we used for recruiting, we called an emergency meeting. Klan members crowded around me as I dialed the Watts home.

"I want you to know we're coming to get you," I hissed when the reverend answered. "And this time we mean business . . ."

"Hello, Johnny Lee!" he said, as though hearing from a long-lost relative. "You don't have to come for me, I'll meet you. How about at a nice little restaurant I know out on Highway 270? I'm buying."

"This isn't a joke, old man. We're coming over and when we're finished, you'll wish you'd never crossed us."

"This place has the best home cooking you ever tasted. Apple pie that'll make you long for more. Fluffy mashed potatoes. Iced tea in mason jars . . ."

I slammed down the phone. "He wants to take us out to dinner," I said in disbelief. "Talked about apple pie and iced tea."

"The old man's gone crazy," someone said. "Let's forget about him."

We left Reverend Wade Watts alone after that. I turned my energies to solidifying my position in my "family," and in 1989 I was appointed Imperial Wizard. I had just gone through a divorce and lost custody of my baby daughter, and in desperation I focused on a new goal. I wanted to unify all hate groups—from skinheads to neo-Nazis—under the umbrella of the Klan. I arranged a national meething where those groups would meet and, I hoped, united in strength.

That was to be the culmination of my efforts. But on the day of the gathering, the Klan, skinheads and neo-Nazis all started fighting, accusing one another of stealing their members and mailing lists. By the time I arrived, my unity meeting was in shambles. As I looked out over the stormy proceedings, I realized: these groups wanted to "purify" the world and have it all be like them—but they hated one another. Did I really want to live in a world of people like that?

Were those the people I wanted to be my family? A family whose hate extended to all colors, backgrounds, and ages. Even babies like Reverend Wade Watts's little daughter Tia. "How can you hate this child?" he had asked.

How far I had come from the days when I sang those words: "Jesus loves the little children, all the children of the world; red and yellow, black and white, they are precious in His sight . . ."

Suddenly I was repulsed by the poison that swirled around me. I felt sick to my stomach. I turned in disgust and walked out the door. Eventually I told the other Klan officials I was giving up my position and leaving the group forever.

My life was a wreck. As the weeks passed, filled by a sense of shame and worthlessness, I fell into deep depression—and the stultifying numbness of alcohol. Then came the terrible day I found myself in my shabby apartment raising a loaded gun to my head. *Daddy, I'm following in your footsteps. There's no other way to go . . .*

I was about to pull the trigger when I saw sunlight break through the partially closed blinds—and onto a Bible that lay gathering dust on my bookshelf, an old

Bible like the one I had seen my grandmother read so many times. Maybe there is another way. I put down the gun and picked up the Bible. It fell open to Luke 15—the parable of the prodigal son. I read the story three times, then I fell on my knees and wept.

I quietly joined a church—whose congregation was multiracial—and kept a low profile, studying the Scriptures, getting grounded in God's Word. Two years passed. And finally in 1991 I made a phone call I had to make.

"Reverend Watts?" I asked when he picked up.

He knew my voice right away. "Hello, Johnny Lee," he said warmly.

"Reverend Watts, I . . . I want you to know that I resigned from the KKK two years ago. I gave my heart to Jesus and I'm a member of an interracial church."

"Praise the Lord!" he shouted. "I've never stopped praying for you! Would you do me the honor of speaking at my church?"

How can he forgive me? How could he have cared about me all those years?

When I stepped to the podium at his church and looked out over the congregation of mostly black faces, I told my story simply, not hiding from the past or sugar-coating the depth and bitterness of my involvement. Then I told them how God had changed all the hate in my heart to love.

There was silence when I finished. A teenage girl got to her feet and ran down the aisle toward me, arms open. I started to move in front of the altar, to pray with her. As I passed the reverend, I realized he was weeping. "Don't you know who that is, Johnny Lee?" he asked quietly. "That's Tia. That's my baby."

Yes, what I needed was a real family. And there had been one waiting to open its arms to me all along.

The Woman Who Cooked Me Breakfast

RILEY ARCENEAUX

Desperate. That's what I was that February morning in 1984 when I peered through the window of Louise Degrafinried's house. Hungry, cold—and dangerous. It had been three days since I'd busted out of prison. I was a convicted murderer on the run, my finger on the trigger of a stolen shotgun.

To many of you, this story probably sounds familiar. In the October 1984 issue of *Guideposts*, Louise Degrafinried described how I broke into her house and held her and her husband, Nathon, hostage. At least, I tried to. I doubt anybody could ever tell that woman what to do. She took one look at me, stared down the barrel of my shotgun and said, "Son, put that gun away. We don't allow violence in this house. This is God's house."

She cooked me breakfast—the first home-cooked meal I'd had in four years. Then, as I ate, she prayed for me. Nothing special. She just asked God to protect me and to help me find peace and forgiveness. Tears rolled down her cheeks—not of fear, but of pity and love. Mrs. Degrafinried convinced me to give myself up. She even held my hand and walked me to the waiting police cars to make sure I didn't get hurt.

But my story didn't end there. Something happened to me that morning around the kitchen table. A seed of love was planted deep in my heart. Over the next few years, Mrs. Degrafinried nourished that seed with phone calls and letters to me in prison. I tried to escape one more time, but I was caught and thrown into solitary confinement. It was in that hole—that hell on earth— that I really began to think about Mrs. Degrafinried's courage and compassion in the face of hatred—my hatred. Where did that kind of courage come from?

Mrs. Degrafinried and I wrote back and forth for a long time. Her handwriting was shaky due to arthritis, but her words were always strong and clear. "I believe in you. Trust God to work in your life. Be patient, study your Bible and look for the good in everybody."

Faith, I realized. Faith was the answer to my question. In 1995 I was granted parole, thanks in part to testimony by Mrs. Degrafinried. One of the first things I did was go visit her in that little country house I remembered so vividly. When she saw me at the screen door, a big smile broke across her face.

"It's Riley!" Mrs. Degrafinried exclaimed and enfolded

me in an enormous hug. That time, I was the one who cried.

I found work at an awning company. My wife, Alice, whom I met on visitors' day in prison, is executive director of Reconciliation Ministries, a nonprofit support group for the families of prisoners. We collect food and presents to give to the kids at Christmas and on birthdays and keep a house near the prison where visiting families can stay for free. I also counsel inmates about adjusting to life once they're released, and speak to their children and spouses.

Louise Degrafinried passed away in 1998 at age eighty-seven. Her children asked me to speak at her funeral and be a pallbearer. I was honored. Not long after, her daughter, Ida Marshall, a principal, asked me to address students at her elementary school.

I got up in front of all those young people and told them my story and about the bad choices I'd made. Then I talked about the good choices and about courage, the kind of courage that Louise Degrafinried had shown me. Its goal isn't to hurt, but to change hearts. I should know. It changed mine.

The Road to Freedom

HOLLY BAXLEY

As my husband and I rounded the corner into the dining area of the sandwich shop, I suddenly halted, startled by the scene before me. A group of men were joking and laughing as they ate their submarine sandwiches. One person in particular really fascinated me. Before I could talk myself out of it, I approached his table.

"May I take your picture?" I inquired.

"Now?" he barked at me.

"Why not?" I countered back.

Reluctantly, he nodded his consent. I tried to capture the casual atmosphere of the sandwich shop, which contrasted against the group's ornate implements and impressive military uniforms that seemed so out of place, and might I add, out of date as well.

After I took their picture, I gave the digital camera to my husband. His eyes twinkled with mirth as he gazed at the spectacle caught on the camera. He handed it back to me so I could see the picture too. It was so funny, I thought it would make a great advertisement for the sandwich shop.

Where does the 'Napoleon of the West' go to eat after he's had a hard day besieging the Alamo? Why, he and his compadres eat at . . .

"Holly? Are you ready?"

My mind was pulled back from my daydream by the call of Brent's voice. He had pulled open the door to the sandwich shop and was holding it for me. I glanced back at the elite militia group and waved my thanks. Santa Anna and his *generals* waved in return and went back to attacking their subs.

Okay, so they were re-enactment actors, but their uniforms were right off the pages of history. And now I had them captured on my camera to document what I thought would be the randomness of such an encounter.

Brent grabbed my hand and we stepped out into the sunshine as we continued to enjoy the city of San Antonio and our nineteenth wedding anniversary. We soon realized that our run-in with Santa Anna wasn't just mere chance.

As we walked toward the Alamo, we passed school groups, Girl Scout troops, a Mexican garrison, casual tourists, Tennessee Volunteers, and genteel women in gingham. We approached the front lawn to find Colonel William Travis deep in conference with Davy Crockett, while Jim Bowie talked with a contemporarily dressed announcer to our right.

It turned out that we had planned our anniversary

trip on the same weekend as the annual reenactment of the Battle of the Alamo. It just seemed so surreal, watching the past and present collide together in such a happy, celebratory way.

But then again, celebrating our anniversary at all was very surreal as well.

To understand this, I need to take you back almost a year prior to Brent's and my anniversary. The occasion was not a happy one. In fact, for all practical purposes it should have been the end of our marriage.

Four deacons sat in our living room to explain to me why they were asking my husband to resign his pastorate at our church. I sat stunned, then angry, then devastated as they informed me that they had been monitoring his computer activity, and had proof that he had been with someone else.

I was too shocked to cry, though the tears threatened to slip down my cheeks. I looked over at my husband and he looked defeated and devastated as well. Devastated that he had both done what he did and that he had been discovered. And yet, even he would tell me later on that he felt relief that it was all out in the open. But deep shame, guilt, and grief overwhelmed him, and he simply could not look me in the eye.

Through the haze of shock, I looked at the mix of emotions that played over the deacons' faces. I had never seen such raw emotions displayed so openly among men before. In such a strange way, it ministered to me as nothing else ever had.

You see, I grew up mainly around women. I knew their feelings very well and how they felt about me. But men were a mystery to me. My dad sporadically appeared in and out of my life, and when he was home, he hid his feelings for me in alcohol. I never could tell if what he was displaying was true feelings or if it was just the booze talking. The only godly men I had in my family life that seemed genuinely concerned for my well-being, were my wonderful brother-in-law and my husband—my knight in shining armor.

As I looked at Brent that night, I no longer saw a knight, but a defeated, broken man. At the same time, these four amazing men were ready to do battle for me! They looked as if they had their swords drawn, ready to fight all of hell if necessary for my honor and dignity. Never had I seen such valor among men in such a dark time in my life!

The compassion that poured from them for both of us touched me deeply. While they were stern with my husband, they showed great care and brotherly love for him. They were both angry and sad. Grieved and yet holding out hope.

They didn't have to come over to our house that night. They could have written my husband off, strung him up for public ridicule. They could have decided not to tell me anything and let me rely on Brent to bring this all to light after the resignation. They willingly chose to be there, to face the embarrassment, the anger, the questions, and the tears. They were there to support both of us.

I love them for that, now and forever. They proved their deepest friendship and loyalty to me by being there. In a time when the betrayal should have been the deepest cut to my bleeding heart, somehow each manly presence let me know that someone is always looking out for my heart here on earth. It was as if God was whispering to my soul that there were men who would champion my cause—men who thought I was worth the fight. They were very much God's presence in my life that night, and I will always be grateful to them.

But after they left that night, it seemed as if a living nightmare had begun. We both wanted to wake up and realize it was all just a horrible, horrible dream. But this nightmare wasn't going away. For the first time ever, I contemplated divorcing him. And it shook me to the core of my heart. I fasted and prayed for God to tell me what to do. And bless their hearts, not a single congregational member advocated that I follow through with divorce. In fact, a couple of wonderful members paid for us to go to counseling, as well as provided resources for us to turn to when we got ready to move.

For we had to move. We had no place to live, no funds to pay for a mortgage, and since I was a stay-at-home mom, we had no other income. My husband's family graciously offered us a place to stay, and so with heavy hearts and a very fragile, uncertain future, we moved away, leaving behind a devastating mess and taking one with us.

I wondered if I could ever learn to love and trust my husband again. I had forgiven him, but I was so upset that I could not forget. Every time I would try to forget, the deep hurt and pain would resurface, and I'd find myself fighting anger and frustration. He was doing everything he could do to show his repentance and his deep love for me for not leaving, and yet it was never enough.

I had heard it said that resentment is like drinking poison and waiting for the other person to die. And I knew that if I kept up in this anger and hurt, eventually it really would not only poison my soul but my very physical body as well. I begged God to help me let this go. Help me forget.

But that's not what He did. Instead He gave me an object lesson I'll never forget.

One day I was closet cleaning and came across a toy ax, which just didn't sit right with me. It came from a previous family member who lived in our home before we did. Just looking at it gave me chills. It was made of plastic and rubber, and with the original owner it was used as Halloween decoration and then went back into the dark of the closet. I decided that I didn't want it in our home, nor did I want my son to play with it.

So, since the ax had a plastic handle, I thought I'd just bend the thing, stick it in the trash, and get on with cleaning. I guess it was older than I originally thought for the plastic was brittle, and it broke off in my hands into many jagged pieces. It was like shrapnel and left my left hand and forearm scared and bleeding.

Still, as I was cleaning up the mess on the floor, I thought of the scripture in Isaiah 54:17 (NASB) that says, "No weapon formed against you will prosper . . ." I felt very smug as I thought about the destruction of this toy and that scripture. But as I looked down at my bleeding hand, I thought *Yeah, but it still hurts.*

And that's when I felt this still small voice in my heart whisper, *You seemed to think that prevailing in this life meant that you wouldn't get hurt, but that's not what I've ever told you. I never promised you that you wouldn't get hurt in this life. I promised you that the weapons in your life would not prevail against you. You'll still get wounded, you'll still hurt, but it won't knock you down and defeat you. You will rise up in Me, and I will heal you, for I promised you that. And I promised you that no weapon formed against you would prevail and win.*

I began to cry, not because my hand was hurt, but because the truth of that statement just soaked in my soul. How many times in the name of forgiveness have I tried to bury the hatchet only to leave the handle sticking back out so I could grab it at will and wield it against whoever was hurting me at the time?

Quickly I told Brent about what happened with the ax and what God showed me in that. He looked at me in love and said, "Wow, God is showing me something in that too. Breaking the handle is like true forgiveness. It is not only burying the hatchet, but shattering the very thing that would keep us from truly forgiving and not allowing us the stronghold of picking it back up. But true forgiveness also comes with a price. It hurts and cuts us in the process. But Jesus promised to heal, because He is faithful. And once that handle's gone, it's gone forever."

We sat still together and just let it soak into both of us. It was the catalyst that got us to talking earnestly about sin and forgiveness, fallen nature and grace. The resentment I held over him shattered that day in my heart, just like the ax handle in my hand. Yes, it hurt, but Jesus promised to heal, and I knew He was faithful and true to His Word.

Over time, the love and trust started returning. We learned to laugh and love again. While there were many hard days alone crying and receiving healing, there were just as many days of just being bathed in Jesus's love, through the study of His word, and through encouraging words of friends that God strategically placed in our lives.

That following spring, when we celebrated our anniversary in San Antonio, it was if God just poured out the charm of the city on us. We watched as the city embraced the pain of its own devastating anniversary and turned it into something truly beautiful in remembering the Alamo and those who stood against adversity and all odds in the name of freedom. As we strolled down the beautiful and romantic Riverwalk in the evening, we watched the street lights make the Guadeloupe River sparkle and shimmer. And I realized the heartache and great sacrifice of the few, paved the way not just for the peace of their children, but for generations to come.

I felt Brent look down at me, his hand wrapped tightly around mine. His eyes reflected the light and they seemed to shimmer too. We embraced as the city slowly walked around us. We, too, were standing against the odds, and our road to forgiveness and freedom was finally beginning.

Beyond Forgiveness

LIZ PARROW

Wade's foot tapped a nervous rhythm under the table where we sat at the front of the auditorium at Moorhead State University. The audience of college students had fallen silent after the moderator's introduction, and I could feel the air practically quiver with tension as they waited to hear what the young man beside me had to say.

Wade's a big guy, over six feet tall, with a football player's build, but he looked like a scared little kid all hunched over in his chair. His shirt collar was still damp from the cold water he'd splashed on his face—to calm his nerves, he'd said, but judging from the beads of perspiration trickling down his forehead, it hadn't helped. I gave his hand a quick squeeze as he raised the microphone. He opened his mouth to speak, but no sound came out.

He cleared his throat and tried again. "I'm Wade Pfarr," he said, his voice barely above a whisper. "Because I got drunk and then got behind the wheel, two good people are dead. Because of me, Liz will never see her husband and daughter again . . . "

I thought back to when I lived in Perley, Minnesota, back to that Saturday afternoon six months earlier, the last time I saw Don and Becky alive. That day, August 1, 1998, had been a long one at the nursing home where I worked the early shift, and I felt myself dragging a bit as I headed home. But my tiredness lifted as soon as I walked in our front door and laid eyes on my husband and daughter. Don gave me a big smile.

"Hi, hon!" he said, tipping his cowboy hat. Becky flashed me a grin just like her daddy's.

"Hey, Mom, we were just leaving for music practice," she said, picking up her guitar case. She and Don were part of the country-gospel group that played during services at our church. "Catch up with you tonight?"

"Sure," I replied. "I'll be up late studying anyway." I was taking classes toward my R.N. degree. "Bye, Donny." His mustache tickled my cheek when we kissed. I gave Becky a hug. "Bye, Beck. I love you."

I waved from the front window as they headed off in our pickup toward church, just across the state line in West Fargo, North Dakota. After dinner, I hit the books. Around midnight, when Don and Becky weren't home yet, I decided to turn in. *Those two,* I thought, climbing into bed. *They get into their music and totally lose track of time.*

A few hours later I woke up. They still weren't back. *Something's wrong.* When I heard a truck pull into our driveway, I ran to the front door and threw it open. But it was Don's brother Harold coming up the walk, and right away I knew. I knew Don and Becky weren't coming back.

"They left without me," I whispered. Don. The love of my life. One of the most giving people I'd ever met. He'd play guitar for the teenagers who hung around the town park, take the time to talk to them because he knew some didn't have fathers at home. Easygoing next to my intensity, stay-at-home to my adventurous, country to my rock 'n' roll—so different from me, and yet such a part of me. And Becky—strong, sunny-tempered, her dad all over again. The only thing bigger than her smile was her heart. She was a music major at Concordia College—played clarinet, sax and guitar, sang like an angel—and was planning to be a teacher.

"Playing music makes me so happy," she'd told me once. "I just want to give kids a chance to feel that joy too."

Don. Becky. Together the three of us had somehow managed to move past our grief at the death of Becky's older brother, Tim, two years before. But now I was all alone. *Lord, how can I go on without them? Who's going to help me heal this time?*

"They died instantly . . . hit by a drunk driver,"

Harold spit out the words. "Some twenty-two-year-old kid. He walked away with only cuts and bruises."

Twenty-two. Just a year older than Becky.

The next afternoon I asked a friend to take me to the lot where our truck had been towed. "Are you sure?" she asked. "The radio said it was pretty bad."

But I had to do it, had to see what had happened to my family. The sheared-off truck cab, twisted metal and bloodstained seats told me more than I wanted to know. Quickly I picked up the few things of Don and Becky's I could—some cassette tapes and guitar picks, Becky's makeup compact. When my fingers touched the soft felt of Don's cowboy hat, my loss hit me so hard, I doubled over.

Are you ready to forgive?

The words cut through my pain. I didn't know if I'd heard the voice or sensed it, but I knew unmistakably who it was.

God, how can you ask that of me when I'm hurting this much? Clutching Don's hat, I turned away and hurried to my friend's car.

The next day I was on my way home from making funeral arrangements when I was drawn irresistibly to the scene of the accident. Near the junction of Highways 10 and 75 I parked by the roadside and got out of my car. Maybe if I stood where Don and Becky had died, I could feel them with me one last time.

Slowly I walked east along the shoulder of Highway 75, tracing their route. At the intersection with 10, I looked north, the direction from which the drunk driver had come barreling through. I could imagine Don and Becky blinded by the blazing lights of his truck right before he hit them, their last seconds filled with terror. God, they deserved better. I can't . . .

Suddenly I heard the sounds of people talking, laughing. Where'd that come from? No one else was on the roadside.

Mom, it's okay. Dad, Beck and I are happy to be together.

That had to be Tim. But how—?

Liz, that driver . . . he's just a kid.

Donny. I'd know his voice anywhere.

You can forgive him and let people really see God at work.

Mom, Becky's voice harmonized with her dad's like always, *you forgave me all my mistakes. He must be hurting too.*

That was Don and Becky for you, their hearts big enough to go out even to the young man who'd cut their lives short. I didn't think I had that kind of love in me, especially not now, but maybe if I tried to be more like Don and Becky, I could feel farther from my grief and closer to them. "I can't do it on my own, God," I prayed. "You'll have to give me the strength to forgive."

A few weeks after the funeral, I caught the end of a news update on TV. A tall, husky young man was being led out of the courthouse, head bowed. I couldn't see his face, but he was identified as Wade Pfarr, the drunk driver who'd caused the accident. Something about the way he carried himself, his broad shoulders hunched, the back of his neck exposed and vulnerable, reminded me of my own son when he knew he'd done something wrong.

Don and Becky were right. Wade was just a kid, and he looked to be hurting too, maybe as much as I was. At least people were sympathetic to my pain. Already I'd heard the whispers, the harsh judgments that would trail Wade wherever he went from now on. "I never thought I'd be asking you this, God, but please let there be some understanding for Wade," I said. "This tragedy has ruined enough lives."

About six weeks after the accident, a friend of Wade's called me. "Wade would like to tell you how sorry he is in person. I know it's a lot to ask, but will you consider meeting him?"

Warily I agreed to see Wade at my church that weekend. When we met face to face after the service and I saw the tears coursing down his cheeks, I felt not anger but compassion.

"I'm sorry, Mrs. Parrow," he murmured. "I'm so sorry." He hung his head.

"Wade, look at me," I said.

Slowly he lifted his head and even more slowly raised his eyes to meet mine.

"There's something I think you need to know," I said. "God has forgiven you. And so will I."

Wade cried harder. "I don't deserve it," he sobbed. "How can you forgive me when I've taken so much from you?"

I reached out and took his hand. "Only through God."

Wade's eyes searched my face with a kind of desperate longing, as if he couldn't quite believe what I'd said, but wanted to. And I found myself hoping that one day he would come to understand what I meant.

Slowly I went about putting my life back together, keeping busy with work and church. The hardest thing was not having anyone waiting for me when I came home. The house used to be so alive with Don and Becky's music and laughter, but now all I heard was the hollow echo of my own footsteps. I tried to fill the emptiness with prayer. "Lord," I'd ask for Wade and me both, especially after he told me he'd pled guilty to vehicular manslaughter and was facing a sentence of up to twenty years in jail, "show us how to make our way through this ordeal. Help us find the good."

On Christmas Eve, four days before his sentencing hearing, Wade and I met for coffee at a local Denny's restaurant. He looked drawn, tired.

"What's wrong?" I asked.

"My grandfather died," he said. "I thought nothing could be worse than my sister passing in May, but . . . " Wade caught himself. "What am I saying? This can't even compare to what I put you through . . ."

"Don't," I interrupted. "We've both lost so much this year. Maybe it's time to help each other move beyond the pain."

Wade stared at me. "Liz, how can you be so strong?"

"But I'm not," I said. "This is a struggle for me too. God's the one who is strong."

Wade nodded, his gaze turning thoughtful.

At his hearing, I was among several people—including his boss and some of his high-school teachers—to speak up for him. We told the judge that Wade had made a tragic mistake and asked him to give Wade a chance to redeem himself. The judge heard us. Wade was sentenced to eighteen months in county jail with release for work and community service.

Before the judge assigned him to a specific project, an opportunity came up for Wade to serve our community in a way only he could. A student group at local Moorhead State University saw the media coverage of the hearing and asked if Wade and I would speak at the school about the dangers of drinking and driving.

"I want to, but I don't know if I can," Wade admitted when I relayed the request to him. "I get real nervous if I have to get up and talk in front of people."

"I'll be right there with you," I reassured him.

He was quiet for a minute. "I have to try," he said. "If we reach just one kid, it'll be worth it, right?"

I looked into his eyes and nodded. "You can do this, Wade."

Backstage at Moorhead State the day of the presentation, Wade was literally shaking from nerves. I took his hands.

"Lord," I prayed aloud, "give Wade the strength you have given me."

"Amen," Wade whispered.

We stepped onstage and took our seats in front of the packed auditorium. And then, along with the audience, I listened to Wade tell his story.

"I was partying at my friends' wedding reception. I don't usually drink, so I didn't realize how messed up I was," Wade said. "I figured I was okay to drive home. But the next thing I knew, paramedics were pulling me out of my truck. A police officer told me I'd hit another vehicle and killed two people . . . "

Wade's voice broke, and he had to take a deep breath before he went on to tell about being booked at the police station, getting sentenced, having to ask people to drive him to and from work because his license had been revoked, spending his nights and weekends in jail, and living with the knowledge that his bad decision took two lives.

"Next Liz is going tell you about Don and Becky, the family she lost that night. Many lives, not just my own, will never be the same. Please, don't make the same mistake I did. Don't drink and drive. Ever."

When Wade finished his speech, I felt a familiar warmth fill me. It took me a moment to recognize what it was. That mixture of love and pride I'd felt listening to Becky play a solo at one of her concerts. *Beck, thank you,* I told her silently. *I guess you and your dad knew the only way for me to move on and really live again was to take that first step and forgive.*

Since then, Wade and I have spoken to hundreds of students in Minnesota and North Dakota, telling them what can happen if they mix alcohol or drugs with driving. We have become good friends, Wade and I, and I look forward to our talks every week when I drive him to and from his job. Watching him grow in his faith, grow as a person, has brought me more joy than I imagined was possible after I lost my family.

When Wade tells me, "You've taught me so much about God," I know that somewhere the faces of my own best teachers, Don and Becky, are lit up with matching smiles. And I know that together, Wade and I have moved beyond the tragedy that first joined us, beyond even forgiveness, to the healing only God's love can bring.

Finding Life on Death Row

SUE NORTON

Sue Norton lives in Arkansas City, Kansas. She received terrible news during a phone call from her brother in January 1990. Her much beloved daddy, Richard Denny, and his wife, Virginia, were found murdered in their home. Sue's daddy was shot to death in his isolated Oklahoma farmhouse. The crime netted the killer $17.00 and an old truck.

Sue says she felt numb. She couldn't understand why someone would want to hurt people who were old and poor. The loss of her daddy just broke her heart.

Sue sat through the trial of Robert Knighton (B. K.). She was confused about how she should feel. She tells me that everyone in the courtroom was consumed with hate. They all expected her to feel the same way. But she couldn't hate the way they did because she says, "It didn't feel good."

The last night of the trial she knew there must be

another way. She couldn't eat or sleep that night and prayed to God to help her. When morning came, she had this thought: *Sue, you don't have to hate B. K.; you could forgive him.*

The next day, while the jury was out for deliberation, Sue got permission to visit B. K. through the bars of his holding cell. Sue relates, "I was really frightened. This was my first experience in a jail. B. K. was big and tall; he was shackled and had cold steely eyes."

At first B. K. refused to look at Sue. She asked him to turn around and he answered, "Why would any one want to talk to me after what I have done?"

Sue replied, "I don't know what to say to you. But I want you to know that I don't hate you. My grandmother always taught me not to use the word 'hate.' She taught me that we are here to love one another. If you are guilty, I forgive you."

B. K. thought Sue was just playing games. He couldn't understand how she could forgive him for such a terrible crime. Sue says, "I didn't think of him as a killer, I thought of him as a human being."

People thought Sue had lost her mind. Friends would step to the other side of the road to avoid her. But Sue says, "There is no way to heal and get over the trauma without forgiveness. You must forgive and forget and get on with your life. That is what Jesus would do."

B. K. was put on death row in Oklahoma. Sue often

wrote to him and visited him occasionally. She felt that B. K. should never leave prison, but she didn't want him executed. She had become friends with B. K. and because of her love and friendship he became a devout Christian.

Sue believes that some good has come out of her Daddy's death and says, "I have been able to witness to many people about Jesus and forgiveness and helped others to heal. I have brought B. K. and many other men on death row to our Lord Jesus Christ. I live in peace with my Lord!"

The Circle of Forgiveness

B. J. TAYLOR

I hate this school. And I hate your stupid rules," I'd muttered.

"We have rules for a reason, miss, and you have to learn to follow them," the principal said.

He scribbled on the papers in front of him. I read it upside down—*One Week Suspension*. That wasn't going to look so great on my school records, but what did I care? This had been the third school in three years. A middle school with the stupidest rules I'd ever seen. Who knew leaving school grounds in the middle of the day would be such a big deal?

I was just hungry and there was a Burger King right around the corner. *I'll only be a minute,* I reasoned. When I pushed open the side door and dashed out, something in my head told me I was making a mistake, but I didn't care. Why should I care about that school or any other? I probably wouldn't be there long anyway.

I wished we'd never moved back to Wisconsin. We'd gone to Arizona a year and a half before and I'd finally made some friends. Then one night Dad sat all of us kids down at the kitchen table. "We're moving back. The business isn't going well. We'll go in shifts—you girls first and then your mom and I will follow with your younger brother."

I couldn't believe it. Moving again. Away from the friends I'd made. Where I had finally felt accepted.

Now, two months into the new school year, I couldn't figure out what assignment we were working on or what the homework was. And I was sick of living with my aunt whose house smelled like Lysol.

Then Mom and Dad got back from Arizona and rented an apartment. We were all crammed into a small space with no room to breathe.

"You're grounded," Dad said when he found out about the suspension. "You can't leave the house for a week."

"You've got to be kidding," I'd said. "What am I going to do around here?"

"You can help your mother unpack."

"Yeah, right. Like that's what I want to do."

"Don't sass back. This move has been hard on all of us," Dad replied.

"It's been a lot harder on me!" I shouted and then ran up to the tiny bedroom I shared with my two sisters. I threw myself on my bed and sobbed. Nobody cared. Nobody.

The next day was Saturday, and then Sunday went

by fast. On Monday morning I was bored. "Mom, can't I go over to the mall or something?" I was just twelve but almost thirteen. I wanted cool clothes, shoes, and a new backpack like the other kids had.

"I'm not taking you to the mall. But I am taking you to your grandmother's house," Mom said. "Your dad and I talked about it. Your grandma said you're welcome to come over there and stay with her while you're home from school."

"You're kidding, right? Grandma is like so old. What am I going to do at her house?"

"She'll think of something," Mom said.

There was no arguing with Mom. Later that morning, with my younger brother buckled into his car seat in the back, Mom drove me to my grandmother's house. It was a long ride and I had time to think. I'd fight any suggestions Grandma had. Why should I be nice to someone so old? She couldn't possibly understand what I was going through.

"Hi there, Barbie," Grandma said when she opened the door. "Come on in. I've got lots of fun things planned."

"I think I'll just watch TV if that's okay with you," I said.

"That's not okay with me. We're going to do things together."

"Whatever," I replied.

Mom left, saying she'd be back that night to pick me up. I couldn't wait.

"We have some laundry to fold," Grandma said. "Why don't you come and help me?"

"Nah. You do it. I'm tired," I said.

"Tired? A young girl like you? Grab the towels out of the dryer and bring them here. We'll fold them together."

I walked into the small laundry room and opened the dryer. Filling my arms with warm, fluffy towels, I inhaled the aroma of fresh laundry soap. Grandma's house always smelled fresh. "Here ya go," I said as I plopped them down on the couch.

"Sit beside me and help me fold," she said.

What could I do? I was stuck here for the whole day. After the towels were folded, Grandma said it was time to clean up the breakfast dishes. So we did those and then she got stuff out of the fridge for lunch. We made sandwiches of lunch meat and cheese, and she poured me a big, tall glass of milk.

"A growing girl like you needs a healthy dose of milk and maybe even some cookies for dessert."

Now that's what I was talking about. We rarely had any sweets in our house lately. "These are good, Grandma," I had to admit when she handed me the plate.

"Oh, you like them? Maybe we'll make some together later this week."

I guessed that would be okay. Why not? Anything to pass the time.

Later that afternoon, we played Go Fish. Before I knew it the clock's hands approached five o'clock and Mom was at the door to pick me up.

"Bye, Barbie. See you tomorrow," Grandma called out sweetly as I got in the car.

"How was your day?" Mom asked when we were on the way home.

"Fine," I replied. I still wasn't sure how I felt about being with my old grandmother, but I wasn't going to tell my mom we had any fun either.

The next day Grandma and I played Yahtzee and Clue. And she let me help her chop up liver into tiny pieces after she cooked it up for her Chihuahua, Princess. "Grandma, why don't you just feed her canned dog food, or the hard dry stuff? Why do you go to all this trouble?"

"Because she's special. And I like to treat her nice," Grandma replied.

I didn't see the sense in it, but hey, it was Grandma's dog.

The third day, Grandma had all the stuff out to make homemade cookies. It was fun to watch them bake in the oven and decorate them with sugar. She even let me eat some warm ones.

"So what's going on with school?" she asked between bites.

"Oh, nothin'," I replied.

"It's not nothing when you get suspended. Tell me what happened."

"School is stupid. No one understands. I'm all alone again and don't fit in." I grabbed another cookie and took a long drink of milk.

"You're not alone, sweetheart, and your mom and dad are trying their best."

"They're not the ones that have to walk into a new school. I have no idea what's going on in class and everyone stares at me. I feel so different from everybody else. And I don't have any friends."

"I know all about being different and not having friends, too. Your grandpa died when you were just a baby. All my friends had husbands, and I was alone. They didn't invite me to get-togethers anymore. It hurt."

"What did you do?" I asked.

"I got busy doing things that made me happy. I crocheted blankets for all of you grandkids; I joined the church down the road; and I helped out with the potluck dinners. Everybody loved my cooking."

I stuffed another cookie into my mouth. She was right about that.

"Life is what you make of it, Barbie. You can be mad

at the world because of the way things are, or you can turn yourself around and decide to make the best of it."

"Like you did?" I said.

Grandma smiled. "Want to play Checkers?"

"Sure, but can I have one more cookie, please?"

"You bet. You can have all you want. You're special. And you are never alone. Remember, God loves you, and your parents love you, even if life is hard sometimes."

"I know God loves me, Grandma. I hear that in church every Sunday." I took my plate to the sink. "But why did Dad have to move us back here? I was happy in Arizona."

"Your dad told me how hard it was to make the decision to move again," Grandma said. "He's doing the best he can, sweetheart. It's not easy trying to make enough money to support a growing family."

I thought about how hard Dad worked. How much he wanted to give Mom and us kids nice clothes to wear and good food to eat. It wasn't his fault that we had to move back. And maybe if I didn't walk around school with my head hanging down I'd make more friends. Maybe if I smiled at others they'd smile back.

"Mom and Dad are trying their best, huh?" I asked.

"Yup, just like you are. Now grab the Checker board, we have a game to play."

I knew changes wouldn't happen overnight, but I decided to stop having such a bad attitude toward my parents. *Mom and Dad, I'm sorry I've been so hard on you.* I said it in my head and in my heart, I just didn't know if I could say it to my parents yet, but it was a start.

Many years later, when I was married with children of my own, I asked my parents to forgive me for the bad attitude I had during my growing up years. They smiled and said they understood.

Then one day I found myself in the kitchen of my small home with a towering young man of fourteen. He had a pimply face and a voice that was deep one moment and squeaky high the next. He was my grandson, and he had problems of his own.

"Grandma, I hate school, and I hate being told what to do all the time. Mom and Dad are always telling me what to do," he ranted. "Why can't I just do what I want?"

"Here, have some cookies and milk," I said as I poured him a tall, cold glass of milk and passed the plate of chocolate chip morsels toward him. I thought of my grandmother and what she taught me so many years ago. She was gone now, but she was always in my heart.

"I know life is hard sometimes, but your mom and dad are doing their best." I looked at this young man who was struggling through adolescence. He shrugged his shoulders and stuffed another cookie into his mouth.

I knew that eventually he would forgive his parents for the hardships he felt were unjust during his teenage years. It would just take time.

Maybe, when he became a father and then a grandfather, he'd serve a plate of cookies and a tall glass of milk to someone just like him. And the circle of forgiveness would continue.

A NOTE FROM THE EDITORS

This original book was created by the Books and Inspirational Media Division of Guideposts, the world's leading inspirational publisher. Founded in 1945 by Dr. Norman Vincent Peale and his wife, Ruth Stafford Peale, Guideposts helps people from all walks of life achieve their maximum personal and spiritual potential. Guideposts is committed to communicating positive, faith-filled principles for people everywhere to use in successful daily living.

Our publications include award-winning magazines like *Guideposts, Angels on Earth,* and *Positive Thinking,* best-selling books, and outreach services that demontrate what can happen when faith and positive thinking are applied to day-to-day life.

For more information, visit us online at www.guideposts.org, call (800) 431-2344, or write Guideposts, 39 Seminary Hill Road, Carmel, New York 10512.